*Also by George Will*

Statecraft as Soulcraft: What Government Does

The Morning After:
American Successes and Excesses 1981–1986

The Pursuit of Happiness and Other Sobering Thoughts

The Pursuit of Virtue and Other Tory Notions

# THE
# NEW
# SEASON

a spectator's guide to
the 1988 election

George F. Will

SIMON AND SCHUSTER
New York   London   Toronto
Sydney   Tokyo

Library of Congress Cataloging in Publication Data
Will, George F.
The new season.

Includes index.
1. Presidents—United States—Election—1988.
2. Elections—United States.   3. United States—Politics and
government—1981–   .   I. Title.
JK526   1988      324.973'0927      87-20537
ISBN 0-671-60234-9

*For Senator Gordon Allott*

Thanks are owed to Alice Mayhew, my editor at Simon and Schuster, and to Gail Thorin for her grace under pressure (from me). As always, much of my work has been made possible, and all of it has been made easier, by my assistant, the legendary (because infallible) Dusa Gyllensvard.

# CONTENTS

# INTRODUCTION

Prometheus had a hard career. An eagle nibbled his liver for thousands of years. Running for President is sort of like that. To change the analogy only somewhat, presidential candidates, swarmed over and pulled at by staff and press and contributors and, last and sometimes least, the public, know how an artichoke feels when being nibbled to nothingness, leaf by leaf. As this essay is being written, in June, 1987, many political figures are making the preliminary noises and maneuvers that are expected from people in the early throes of running for President. Friendly committees have been organized to be wetted fingers in the Breeze of History and to be, simultaneously, dry fingers on the Pulse of the Republic. In due time each will report that in their fellow, the man and the moment have met. Already clouds of candidates are mixing castigation of rivals with supplication of the distracted citizens of Iowa and New Hampshire. Any candidate setting out to save the Republic from his rivals runs the risk of sounding like Loretta Young addressing Richard the Lion-hearted in the 1935 movie *The Crusades*: "You just gotta save Christianity, Richard! You gotta!" Nevertheless, the candidates will be warning that floodgates of ruin are about to burst, washing society from its foundations, unless voters elevate to glory the one suitable savior.

Yes, indications are rife. There is going to be a presidential election in 1988. Of course, it is not optional. The Constitution is dogmatic about such details. You say we had a presidential election just yesterday? Actually, it was years ago, but time flies when you're having fun.

To an interesting extent and in interesting ways, Americans have been having fun recently. And the 1988 election could and should be wonderfully entertaining, for several reasons, one of which is: All American elections are entertaining. They, like baseball, are dull only to the dull. Pick the supposedly dullest election that comes to mind. Eisenhower versus Stevenson in 1956? Ford versus Carter in 1976? Reagan versus Mondale in 1984? Each of those elections involved large issues, consequential choices, complex personalities; each seems more, not less, interesting as it recedes into the context of the country's rich history. Anyway, how can the orderly disposition of power in a continental nation be other than fascinating?

Presidential elections are among the devices that Americans use to prevent American life from becoming dull. The devices always do that job, and the 1988 election will do it splendidly. It will be the first election since 1968 with no incumbent on the November ballot. In 1968 Lyndon Johnson's decision to retire was not made until the primaries were under way. Thus the 1988 campaign will be the first since 1960 in which everyone knows from the start that both nominations are up for grabs.

So the 1988 election can hardly fail to be even more fascinating than the usual election. But, then, what is a "usual" American election? Back when the earth was young and the Cincinnati Bengals and Cleveland Browns were preparing to play each other for the first time ever, one of the coaches predicted, "It will be a typical Browns-Bengals game." In the same analytic spirit one can note, not entirely facetiously, that the 1988 election will be about what we have come to expect from 1988 elections. Not only are all elections interesting, they are all interesting in different ways. Anyone who thinks he has extrapolated from the welter of events in the recent past some iron law of social development, and who thinks he can therefore distill a crystalline prediction about what will happen on November 8, 1988, is mistaken. He is confused about many things, beginning with the predictive value of political science.

It may well be that when the dust settles after the first Tuesday after the first Monday in November, 1988, it will seem that the outcome was a predictable product of powerful forces discernible years in advance. If so, the forces were not discernible by most of us. As Dizzy Dean declared on the eve of the 1934 World Series between the Cardinals and the Tigers, "This Series is already won, but I don't know by which team."

A wit once defined economics as a science of single instances, meaning, of course, that it is not a science at all. That may be a bit harsh regarding economics, but much the same can be said of the science of studying presidential elections. A favorite way of postulating patterns in politics—patterns that make predictions possible—is to focus on a single variable. A common basis of such monomanias is money. Economic determinism is a hardy perennial in the garden of the social sciences. But the more one knows about real-life flesh-and-blood politics, the less seems explainable in terms of any single variable.

No one knows more about American politics than Michael Barone, a member of the editorial page staff of *The Washington Post* and author of *The Almanac of American Politics*, which has been published biannually since 1973. Just as the Bible is *The Sporting News* of religion, the *Almanac* is the

Bible of American politics. In the 1984 edition of the *Alma-nac*, Barone notes that American politics confounds those analysts who are determined to explain events in terms of such economic variables as personal income:

> Political preferences in the America of the 1940s correlated to a fair degree with income. Republican strength was greater than average in high income states like New York, Connecticut, New Jersey, and Delaware (all of which Thomas Dewey carried over Harry Truman in 1948), while Roosevelt and Truman carried virtually every state with incomes below the national level (the exceptions were rock-ribbed Republican since the Civil War: Maine and Vermont, Nebraska and Kansas). But today there is virtually no correlation between income level and political preference. Utah, with one of the lowest per capita incomes, was the nation's most Republican state in 1980; its low per capita income reflects the large number of children in the state, and family ties and the presence of children began to be correlated with Republican preference by 1980. In the Midwest high income Illinois is more Democratic than low income Indiana; in the East New Hampshire is the most Republican and one of the lowest income states . . . economic factors seem less and less to explain political preference, and cultural variety seems to do it more and more.[1]

Marxists (in America, their political experience is apt to be confined to faculty politics) like to say that politics is an epiphenomenon. That is a Germanic way of saying something that would seem even sillier if not expressed in jargon. To say that politics is an epiphenomenon is to say that political activity is primarily a product of autonomous events and forces rather than the free choices of men and women controlling events and forces. Certainly American politics reflects American life. America always has been, and is now more than ever, a rolling river of change. And, happily, the change is not, by and large, controlled by politics. However, that is just the normal way of things in a free, open society. It does not mean that politics does not matter. One task of politics in a free society is to see that politics remains somewhat peripheral to everyday life. But that does not mean that politics is merely a passive effect of causes somehow more "real." And it does not mean that politics is impotent.

In emphasizing the constancy of change in America, there is a danger of overlooking the great staring fact of our political life: stability. There are 159 nations in the United Nations. How many have not had their form of government changed by internal or external violence since 1914? Seven. (Australia, Canada, New Zealand, South Africa, Sweden, United States, United Kingdom. Costa Rica and Portugal almost make the honors list; they had mild, almost decorous coups. But coups-with-doilies are still coups.) That gross measurement of stability does not begin to gauge the remarkable orderliness of American political competition. Again, Barone:

No other nation has a political system whose basic character has remained unchanged for so long as the United States. We have been holding presidential and congressional elections for 195 years now, and in that time just 39 men have held our highest office. The senior senator from New Hampshire still sits at Daniel Webster's desk; the inkwell is kept filled and sand is provided for blotting. Our political parties, though not mentioned in the Constitution, are nearly as old. The Democratic Party was formed in the early 1830s, under Andrew Jackson's aegis, by that master politician Martin Van Buren; the Republican Party sprung up almost spontaneously in reaction to Stephen Douglas's Kansas-Nebraska Act of 1854 and won the congressional elections that year. The two have remained our major parties ever since.[2]

Much of the drama of American political experience is the combination of cultural dynamism and institutional stability. The latter has become more remarkable as the former has become more pronounced. There has been what some perceive as mild instability in the central office of American government, the presidency. Prior to Reagan there had been no two-term Presidents since Eisenhower, and not since Franklin Roosevelt has a party elected a President twice and then held on to the office in the next election. The last such achievement before FDR was in the elections of McKinley (1896, 1900) and Theodore Roosevelt (1904).

However, the fact betokens neither systemic instability nor volatility in the electorate. In that period there have been two assassinations (McKinley, Kennedy), two deaths in office (Harding, FDR), one incapacitating illness (Wilson), one Depression, two world wars, two other large wars (Korea, Vietnam), a civil rights revolution, a revolution in communications, the transformation of the nation from an agricultural to an urban industrial society. The wonder is that the only detectable political instability is the inability of either political party to hold the presidency for a full generation.

Candidates reflect changes in political fashions. Stephen Hess of the Brookings Institution notes, "Between 1824, when Andrew Jackson first ran for President, and 1892, when Benjamin Harrison last ran for President, generals were nominated in all but three elections (1844, 1860, 1884). In this century just World War II yielded a nominee, Dwight D. Eisenhower."[3] And Eisenhower seemed to be the most civilian of the military heroes. The most military of the lot, Douglas MacArthur, was a damp squib as a presidential candidate in 1952. Today the Senate is the most fertile source of candidates, but in the post-war period only one person (John Kennedy) has gone directly from the Senate to the White House. Before he did it, the last person to do it was Warren Harding. Perhaps that means that the odds are against a Senator winning in 1988. Or perhaps it means that a successful candidacy by a Senator is (as optimistic baseball fans say when their team sends a .230 hitter to the plate) "overdue." Or maybe it means nothing.

In any case, the purpose of this volume is not to predict the outcome of the 1988 election. Nor is its purpose to say who ought to win. Rather, its purpose is the more modest one of clarification. It offers thoughts about how to think about what the candidates will be thinking about and doing. It is a spectator's guide to the civic spectacle now unfolding.

I do not use the word "spectacle" disparagingly. A presidential election has its circus-like aspects. But the civic conversation of a continental nation is spectacular. And it is a serious business. To understand what the politicians are doing, you must understand what has happened in the politics of the recent past, both electoral politics and the politics of governing. The past has its patterns—patterns, not predestinations, not portents of inevitabilities. The patterns influence the politicians' calculations about the unfolding future.

One of my purposes is to defend the dignity, the gravity, the seriousness of the political vocation. Politics is a serious business not just, or even primarily, because large amounts of time and money and energy and public attention are consumed by it, and not just because the stakes of politics include power, which is serious because it can be the servant of justice or injustice. Politics as American politicians practice it is a serious business also because it is about ideas. So pay attention to the words. The public utterances of politicians, not the private machinations, are the important story.

Various materialist philosophies preach that we are what we eat, or earn, or how we earn, or this or that. Actually, we —individually, and collectively as a nation—are what we say. Richard Brookhiser, managing editor of *The National Review*, is author of a useful book about the 1984 campaign, *The Outside Story: How Democrats and Republicans Re-elected Reagan.*[4] Brookhiser argues that political journalism has become too preoccupied with "inside" stories—the nuts and bolts of political machinery, the wiles and stratagems of hired political guns. As a result, journalism is scanting the "outside story," which concerns the words, themes and ideas that are the most important ingredients in elections. Journalism that neglects the outside story does so for several reasons. One is that a concentration on inside arcana transforms political journalists into a clerisy with privileged access to mysteries. These journalists have the priestly task of mediating those mysteries to laymen. Any theory of social function that exalts those who believe it will not lack believers, so there are many journalists who believe their function is to reveal and decode private mysteries of politics.

A second reason for the preoccupation with the "inside story" is itself a social theory. The "inside story" often turns out to be about the nuances of image-making. And Brookhiser says:

> The disposition to keep one's eye on imagery may derive from a larger social theory, that advertising controls markets. Fifties economists, brooding on tail fins, concluded that Detroit, allied with Madison Avenue, could get anything it wanted. Three decades later, Washington was bailing out Chrysler.[5]

The theory that advertising controls markets is related to the impulse of many professionals to think of themselves as a clerisy. The common denominator of the theory and the impulse is a belief that the public is irrational, or at least only tenuously and intermittently rational. The disposition—and it is a disposition, a character trait—to believe that advertising controls markets carries, of course, an exemption for the person disposed to believe it. No one who believes that advertising manipulates the masses believes that he or she is among the manipulated. Those who believe that advertising controls markets are apt to believe that they—the illuminati who understand what is going on—should serve as shepherds, protecting and guiding the brute herd.

One need not adopt a sentimental assessment of the public in order to insist that, in presidential elections, the voters are, on balance, sensible. That is not to say the electorate invariably makes the wisest choice. Rather, it is to say only—although this is actually quite a lot—that elections are about substantial things, and that most voters know that. Brookhiser's thesis is so sensible that only an age overimpressed with experts and arcana would need reminding of it. His thesis is that in speaking millions of words at thousands of appearances a candidate has a purpose. It is to say something. Looked at this way—looking at the "outside story"—elections no longer seem circuses or brawls or numbing marathons or endless scrums.[6] They seem purposeful, intelligible, even intelligent.

In the famous formulation of Mr. Dooley, Finley Peter Dunne's fictional barkeep, "Politics ain't beanbag." That means politics is not a gentle game. The truth often gets its trousers rumpled and its hair mussed. Politics is not a seminar; it is not a disinterested quest for Truth. It is a passionate quest for power, fame, wealth and—more often than many people think; more often than not—for justice and the public good.

This book is an anticipation of a process that will be rich in unanticipated events and emphases. A presidential campaign is a kaleidoscopic swirl of styles and subjects. But a campaign is not a radical departure from normality. Rather, it is an episode, albeit an intense one, in the continuous conversation of the nation. Therefore campaigns usually do not involve sharp disjunctions in the pattern of the nation's preoccupations. One way, and the necessary way, for a spectator to prepare for informed enjoyment of a campaign is to consider the arguments that for a few years have been agitating people. So this book is an anticipation that nevertheless has, of necessity, retrospective aspects. In it I have drawn upon the thinking and writing I have done as part of the agreeable discipline of writing columns. The craft of writing political columns requires practitioners to monitor the public's agitations. This volume incorporates and elaborates portions of some recent columns about the players and policies that will define the new season.

In this decade, more than in most decades, the political life of the nation has had a focus on one person. So as the curtain rises on 1988, let us set the stage by considering the man who has held the stage in this decade.

# RONALD REAGAN

It has been said that persons are like planets because they carry an atmosphere around with them. Ronald Reagan carried conservatism around with him in the 1970s and 1980s. It was a political atmosphere with a long post-war pedigree. Remember that Reagan, who is often praised (or criticized) for trying to re-establish the complacency (or stability) of the Eisenhower era, was learning to be a conservative in that era.

Eisenhower's smile, writes Jeffrey Hart, "was almost a philosophical statement."[1] The few people who, in the 1950s, wanted to supplement the smile with conservative ideas were casting seeds on stony soil. The emblematic intellectual of the Fifties, Lionel Trilling, had written in *The Liberal Imagination* (1950) ". . . liberalism is not only the dominant but even the sole intellectual tradition."[2] There were, he said, no conservative ideas in circulation. But in 1953 William F. Buckley, Jr., launched the magazine (*The National Review*) that, a quarter-century later, was the President's favorite.

Perhaps in the Fifties the going was good because the

going was easy, and the standards of good were not demanding. We had unchallengeable military superiority, and settled for stalemate in Korea. We had an economic head start on a world recovering from war, and soon were panting.

The infantilism—impatience; hedonism; inability to defer gratification—that produced the cultural dissolution of the Sixties helped give rise to the inflation of the Seventies. Those failings were gathering force in the Fifties. Some of that decade's vitality was license—a letting go after so much bearing down in the Depression and war. The great release of energy in the Fifties had a destructive dimension, reflecting a collapsing capacity for discipline.

The phrase "the Sixties" calls up a montage of vivid images. To many persons the images are tinged with the romance of idealism. To others, myself emphatically included, the images are of almost unrelieved excess. Music was cacophonous, politics was characterized by the self-indulgence of ideologues, even neckties were excessively wide. What almost no one remembers is that some of the first ferments of the 1960s were on the right. The first serious campus disorder was not at Berkeley in 1964, it was at Oxford, Mississippi, in 1962. The first political convention convulsed by the passions of the decade was not at Chicago in 1968 but at San Francisco in 1964, when many Republicans were in a rule-or-ruin mood. In intraparty feuds, tempers can become so foul that each faction decides that, if it cannot win the prize, the prize should not be worth winning.

By the time Goldwater and Rockefeller (and then Scranton) sheathed their knives in 1964, Goldwater could carry only five states. The brawl between Goldwater and Rockefeller was a continuation of the (by then) fifty-two–year war that began between William Howard Taft and Theodore Roosevelt in 1912. Although it was, at its outset, a war about personal ambition—most volcanically, Teddy Roosevelt's—it also was about serious differences that were to define the split between "liberal" (later called "moderate") and "conserva-

tive" Republicans. The crux of the matter was Teddy Roosevelt's exuberant employment of government power for the
purpose of putting a saddle and bridle on the unbridled capitalism that had transformed America in the decades after the
Civil War. Taft represented the conservative tradition identified with a deep-seated distrust of government, especially
when it encroached upon the broad freedom of market forces.

In the growth of conservatism in the post–World War II
period, first came the Word, books such as Russell Kirk's *The
Conservative Mind,* and journals, principally *The National
Review.* It started with a small circulation, but its publisher
knew that *The New Republic* had a circulation of just 33,000
in 1933 when it became a formative influence on the New
Deal.

Then came the Event: The Hiss case mobilized conservatives and gave conservatism an anti-establishment cast. Hiss
was a product of Harvard Law School, a former clerk for Justice Oliver Wendell Holmes, and a splendid example of a
young man destined, or so it seemed, to float to the top of the
Eastern foreign policy establishment. Hiss was tall, thin,
well-tailored. His accuser, Whittaker Chambers, was short,
heavy, rumpled. For both sides in the Hiss case, it was, from
the start and to the finish, "us" against "them." When, during
the 1960 GOP Convention in Chicago, Nixon flew to New
York to reach a platform compromise with Nelson Rockefeller, Barry Goldwater exhorted conservatives to "take this
party back" from "them"—the Eastern establishment. Animus against that establishment was more important than the
fact that Rockefeller's principle demand was for a stronger
defense plank.

F. Clifton White, a Republican activist and consultant, and
William Rusher, publisher of *The National Review,* and
twenty others met in Chicago's Avenue Motel on October 8,
1961. For three years they practiced—actually, they pioneered—the tactics of guerilla warfare in delegate selection.
They activated people who had never before participated in

the process, and took control of the process away from the party leaders. They had a conservative dream—of sawing off the East Coast. The South and West were rising, White reasoned: California's Bank of America had as much money as New York's Chase Manhattan. They nominated an Arizonan.

Goldwater was the last candidate unreconciled to the activist role of the federal government as an engine of distributive justice. (Reagan was only rhetorically unreconciled.) Conservatives had a theory—the "conservatives in the woodwork" theory. Conservatives thought: One reason millions of Americans do not vote is that they are forced to choose between two liberals; give them a choice, not an echo, and conservatives will pour out of the woodwork, into voting booths.

Oh, well. It became another beautiful theory slain by an ugly fact: The outpouring did not happen. But something important had begun to happen with the nomination of Goldwater. Writing in 1965 about the 1964 campaign, Theodore White concluded that Goldwater had defeated Rockefeller for the Republican nomination because Goldwater had "the high moral ground."[3] Rockefeller and then, briefly, William Scranton advertised themselves as "problem solvers" and "moderates," two of the dampest, limpest labels ever affixed to flesh-and-blood candidates in the sweaty arena of politics. "Goldwater," wrote White,

> could offer—and this was his greatest contribution to American politics—only a contagious concern which made people realize that indeed they must begin to think about such things. And this will be his great credit in historical terms: that finally he introduced the condition and quality of American morality and life as a subject of political debate.[4]

In 1964 Goldwater ran rambunctiously, flat-out against government. He got shellacked. But look what has happened since then. In 1968 and in 1972 Nixon won by presenting himself as the voice of the "silent majority" that was being ignored—and when not ignored, trod upon—by "them," meaning the government. In 1976 Carter got to Washington by describing himself as an outsider strange to Washington, and by promising to remain so. His principle promise—a government as good, decent, loving, etc. as the American people —was designed to disparage government while flattering "the people." The 1980 and 1984 elections were won by the man who came to prominence in a 1964 speech that espoused Goldwater's anti-government theme better than Goldwater ever managed to do.

By August, 1974, conservatives had captured the GOP but, it seemed, to no effect: President Ford chose Rockefeller as Vice President. So conservatives decided to win outside the party. Two episodes energized them and proved their potency.

One was the Equal Rights Amendment, which sailed through Congress and then twenty state legislatures in three months, but was defeated by the leadership of one woman, Phyllis Schlafly, whose example dispelled conservative defeatism. A second boost for conservatism came in 1978 when the government threatened to increase regulation of religious schools. Until then many conservatives had flinched from political activism, preferring to pull back in isolation from the national culture. Government regulation of religious schools convinced many hitherto passive conservatives that there was no alternative to political engagement.

Certainly by the late 1970s America was suffering from a sense of . . . well, "malaise" is not too strong a word. However, what was coming was not foreseen.

Suppose that on, say, January 1, 1978, someone had told you that in 1980 not only would the Republicans nominate that elderly ex-actor and retired governor of California—the fellow who could not even beat Jerry Ford, the "accidental President," in the competition for the 1976 nomination. Suppose you also had been told that Reagan would go on to such feats as carrying Massachusetts in two consecutive elections, by comfortable margins. Told that, you would have been, to say no more, skeptical.

If you had been told the same thing at the end of 1978 you still would have been skeptical, but less so. The 1988 election will cap a conservative decade that began with two conspicuous portents, the first coming from California.

Contrary to popular assumption, California is not politically immoderate. Only twice since 1948 has California's vote deviated more than 2 percentage points from the nationwide percentage of presidential winners. In June, 1978, California voters confounded experts and leaders by doing, emphatically, what they had been emphatically told not to do. California voters, who were instructed otherwise by almost every establishment figure and institution, passed Proposition 13, limiting property taxes and heralding an eruption of exasperation with government. California's populist tradition of allowing the electorate to take lawmaking into its own hands is a departure from the core principle of republican government, the principle of representation. That principle is that the people do not decide issues, they decide who shall decide. But because California is a diverse nation in its own right, its referenda can be, as the vote on Proposition 13 was, a leading political indicator for the country.

The second such portent came in the Senate races of 1978, when five liberal Senators were defeated. Three were Democrats beaten in November—Colorado's Haskell, Iowa's Clark, New Hampshire's McIntyre—and one was a Republican, Brooke of Massachusetts. Another Republican, Case of New Jersey, was beaten earlier in the year in a primary. (Democrats won both Republican seats.) This was the first tremor of the earthquake that two years later would produce sixteen Republican freshmen Senators and Republican control of the Senate for the first time since 1954.

In 1978 the Kemp-Roth tax reduction plan was unveiled. This was another indicator of rising conservatism. The plan, melding populist and meritocratic appeals, called for sweeping across-the-board reduction of marginal tax rates. The plan expressed the "supply side" premise that high marginal rates have irrational disincentive effects at all income levels, and that the effects on the wealthy are particularly costly to all levels of society. For people with modest incomes, the rate cuts would enlarge disposable income, thereby expanding their range of comforts and giving a consumption-based push to the economy. For persons of ample means, who probably already were doing their civic duty by consuming to beat the band, the rate cuts would expand both the means and the ardor for investment. The result of this would be job creation, rising productivity and an increase of the supply of goods and services relative to demand. That increase would dampen inflation.

It would be churlish to dwell on the fact that by 1987 the U.S. savings rate was still as dreadful as before the cuts were enacted in 1981. So I will not. Dwell, that is.

Anyway, in 1978 Kemp-Roth was proposed. Two years later, the Republican presidential nominee stood on the steps of the Capitol with other Republican House and Senate candidates, to endorse the plan, which gave his campaign a theme and energy.

In December, 1978, Democrats held a mid-term mini-convention in Memphis, and Edward Kennedy spoke in praise of "sailing into the wind." His speech was a shot across President Carter's bow. Kennedy was making a thinly veiled threat to run against Carter if Carter trimmed to the conservative winds. Carter's reaction was to fight defections on the left by buying off interest groups. He thereby embraced the notion that fidelity to Democratic principles means preserving all programs. Thus, Carter did, in a sense, sail into the wind, and into oblivion.

Actually, a mild conservative wind is not a rarity in the post-war era. The nation was moderately conservative when it chose Eisenhower over Stevenson, twice. Next, it barely preferred Kennedy, a moderate Democrat, over Nixon. Johnson, the only post-Truman President with a Rooseveltian, liberal domestic agenda, was an accident of assassination and the perceived radicalism of his Republican opponent, Goldwater. Two years later Republicans gained forty-seven House and three Senate seats. In 1968 Nixon and George Wallace won, between them, 57 percent of the popular vote. In 1972 Nixon got 61 percent against McGovern. In 1976 the Democrat perceived as the most conservative in the nomination contest (Carter) was nominated and narrowly defeated a conservative Republican, Ford. Then came two conservative landslides. However, the two Reagan landslides differed. In 1980 almost half the eligible electorate did not vote, and almost half of those who did voted against Reagan. He won twelve states (with 135 electoral votes, half the total needed to win) by less than 5 percentage points. He won seven of those by less than 2 percent. In the eight states he won by 5 to 10 percentage points, he got more than 50 percent of the vote in only two (51.2 percent in both Louisiana and Missouri). Granted, that was in a three-person race. But it also was against an exceptionally unpopular incumbent, and the third candidate (John Anderson) got most of his votes at Carter's expense.

Some cranky Americans probably think any President should have a second term so that he cannot escape the consequences of his first term. But it was not a cranky country that conferred a second term. Coming off the "Olympic summer" of 1984, American cheerfulness may have been at a post-war apogee.

Reagan's percentage of the 1984 total vote (58.8 percent) placed just fifth on this century's list of landslides, behind Johnson's 61.1 percent in 1964, Nixon's 60.7 percent in 1972, FDR's 60.8 percent in 1936 and Harding's 60.3 percent in 1920. However, Reagan tied Nixon's record of victories in forty-nine states, and Reagan's 525 electoral votes broke Nixon's 1972 record of 520. Mondale's 13 electoral votes came within a whisker of breaking Alf Landon's record for the fewest electoral votes (8). Mondale got fewer electoral votes than such third-party candidates as Harry Byrd (15 in 1960), Strom Thurmond (39 in 1948) and George Wallace (46 in 1968).

Reagan's electoral record is, as any such smashing achievement is apt to be, a reflection of a distinctive style. In *Cadillac Jack*, a picaresque novel about, among other things, Washington mores, Larry McMurtry describes Washington as "a graveyard of styles," a city of museums in which the defining attitudes are curatorial. There are now five special exhibits in Washington's memory museum of presidential styles. In this century there have been five Presidents whose personalities permeated public life. (I am not including John Kennedy, because he became a permeating presence in the nation's imagination only after, and because of, his death.) Each was followed by someone strikingly different.

The first, Theodore Roosevelt, was the first President recorded by the technology that was a portent of the coming capacity to mass market politicians: motion pictures. TR was, arguably, the most charismatic man ever to occupy the White House. He was succeeded by 300 pounds of anticharisma in the stolid form of William Howard Taft.

The second "permeating President" was Woodrow Wilson. The first sitting President to travel to Europe, Wilson was the first President to rivet his nation's attention by becoming a star on the world stage. There has not since been and probably never again will be anything remotely resembling the adulation he enjoyed during his three-month stay in Europe during the Versailles Peace Conference. The clarity of his ideals, the heat of his passions and the jagged edge of his personality made him an unusually vivid figure to friends and foes. He was succeeded by Warren Harding, a man who, had he been a food, would have been boiled beef: elemental, without flourishes. Harding was, to say no more, not a martyr to an exacting idealism.

The third strong-personality President was Theodore Roosevelt's cousin, Franklin, who brought an aristocrat's élan to a nation desperately in need of infectious confidence. The anomalous nature of his hold on the public imagination was that he demonstrated the compatibility of an elegant manner and an egalitarian appeal. His persona, a product of upper-class advantages, elicited enthusiasm and deference from the bottom of what fancies itself a classless society. In the first election after FDR's death, the loser was another former Governor of New York. The winner was a Missouri machine politician whose personality and manner were severely free of the ornaments of elegance.

The fourth "permeating President," Dwight Eisenhower, in 1960 the oldest person to serve as President, was an avuncular figure who promised and delivered equilibrium. He was succeeded by John Kennedy, the youngest man ever elected President. Kennedy's campaign themes ("Get America moving again," "We can do better," "Vigor" and all that) were calculated to stress a reversal of the Eisenhower manner.

Reagan is the fifth "permeating President" of the age of mass communication. In 1980 the man and the moment met. The nation needed what he delivered—confidence and a sense that government could act decisively (the 1981 tax cuts; the July 7, 1981, defeat of the strike by PATCO, the professional air traffic controllers union; the October 25, 1983, invasion of Grenada) in accordance with a clear vision. This posed a particular problem for Democrats unwilling or unable to rethink their traditional style of presidential campaigning. One Democratic operative came to understand the Reagan difference.

Pat Caddell has played a prominent role—prominence is not a condition from which he flinches—in every Democratic presidential contest since 1972 when, at age twenty-two, he became George McGovern's pollster. He served in a similar role in both Carter campaigns. By 1984, when Caddell was serving Gary Hart, he had some insight into the problem Reagan posed for Democrats.

Caddell said Hart's task in 1984 was to dramatize differences with both the Carter and Kennedy styles of liberalism. But the most telling contrast was between Hart's and Reagan's conceptions of what presidential campaigns should be in the 1980s. Their differences denote different ideas of democratic consent, and leadership.

Gary Hart was an issues-paper politician. He believed in dwelling on details, telling people the particulars of what he planned to do. He believed campaigns should produce consent to programs. Reagan believes campaigns are to fill a reservoir of deference. (If the word "deference" grates on your democratic sensibilities, call it a reservoir of trust.) Reagan favors campaigns that set themes that bolster confidence in the theme-maker's character. His assumption is that the public's attention to politics is intermittent and its attention span is short. A constructive campaign convinces a majority that the candidate is a good fellow with a good idea of what he wants to do. These two perceptions by the public will translate into a lot of latitude for him when the game of governance begins.

In 1988 Republican candidates will be seeking to contrast themselves with Reagan without, Lord knows, seeming in even the slightest way to criticize him. (They will say they want to enlarge upon his larger-then-lifeness, and complete the pilgrimage to perfection that he began, but they will not criticize, which might suggest that there was some slight flaw in some fundamental premise.) It is, therefore, possible that they will become issues-paper politicians, rather as Hart was in 1984.

The year 1988 may not be a good one for anyone's issues-paper campaign. It is possible—I think it is probable—that the most successful Democrats in 1988 will run "thematic" campaigns, as Reagan did in 1984 and as Kennedy did in 1960 (about getting America moving again). This is probable for two reasons. Democrats have not really been happy—seriously happy—since 1960. And a thematic campaign is perfect for a party that cannot say much of anything without causing tantrums somewhere in its ranks or apprehension in the electorate.

Politicians, like the rest of us, tend to believe that the right thing to do is whatever they feel comfortable doing. This is in part because they, like the rest of us, tend to do well what they do comfortably. Most politicians cannot campaign as Reagan did. Reagan's rapport with the public was a rarity. For all who run in 1988, a crucial question will be: Has the public come decisively to prefer Reagan's conception of political leadership? Reagan may have created in the public a preference for a kind of campaigning that few candidates can master.

The kind of campaigning was of a piece with a kind of governing. By setting themes and associating policies with his character, Reagan gave the country the respite it needed after years of strange, prickly, unpredictable personalities (Johnson, Nixon, Carter). When Alexandra saw the corpse of her husband, King Edward VII, she exclaimed: "Now at least I know where he is." That is how Americans felt about the presidency when Reagan settled into it—until the Iran debacle.

Until then, Democrats probably were naming children after a portion of the Constitution: "Come see my bouncing baby boy, Twenty-second Amendment Jones." They rose with the rooster and, before breakfasting (on bran muffins and boysenberry yogurt, you know Democrats), they reread that amendment just for reassurance. Whew! Yes, Reagan must retire in 1989. Democrats were cheerfully generous about Reagan's prowess, like the Dodger pitcher who said of Stan Musial, "I've had pretty good success with Stan—by throwing him my best pitch and then backing up third."

The Iran debacle was especially damaging to Reagan because it struck at his special strength—the perception of him as a man of soothing character and a man of clear convictions (such as: no appeasement of terrorists) so clearly stated that you did not have to hang on his words lest he trick you. Remember how Reagan filled the reservoir of deference: He understood how much the public, with its intermittent attention to politics, craved a President who was such a good fellow, with such a clear idea of what he wanted to do, that the public could tune out and go about its business.

Contrast Reagan's appeal with that of the last Republican elected President before Reagan. Richard Nixon is the only man other than FDR to run for national office (President or Vice President) five times. Nixon has received more votes for President than anyone in American history. One can imagine a typical voter saying to himself or herself in the voting booth: "Nixon is not lovable, probably not even nice. He certainly is not the sort of fellow one wants to be seated next to at dinner. But he does know government, and the world. So I will grit my teeth and pull the lever for him." In contrast, few people voted for Reagan because of any particular practical proficiency. What Reagan is good at is being popular. His popularity is grounded in appreciation of his character traits. People have liked Reagan more for what they know about his character than for what he knows about government and the world. This has been a potent appeal in the 1980s.

Peter Hart and Geoffrey Garin, both Democratic political consultants, have asked focus groups of voters to describe a situation in which they would like to be a "fly on the wall" to observe and judge a candidate. Two answers have recurred. The voters would like to observe a private meeting about political strategy, and the candidate at the family dining table. The latter, according to Hart and Garin, supports their theory that today "the messenger is the message." That is, voters are unusually interested in the candidate's character. The "dining-table" response is the reason that Gary Hart's campaign disintegrated so abruptly.

Most voters agree about what problems are important—the budget deficit, the Soviet Union—but there is no widespread confidence in particular solutions. Therefore voters say: "I am unsure which policy choice should be made, so I concentrate on being sure about the people making the choices."

The preoccupation with character is especially understandable given recent experiences. To repeat, of the four Presidents who immediately preceded Reagan, three were, to say no more, odd. The normal one, Ford, was an accident. By 1980 the country was weary of Presidents who seemed to be working out their private turmoils in public policies.

Reagan's militant normality became a focus of fascination to one of the bright young wits of the Democratic party, Chris Matthews. From his position on the staff of Speaker of the House Tip O'Neill, Chris Matthews studied Ronald Reagan with the close attention that any pedestrian would give to a semitrailer that made a habit of running over his instep. Like many other young Democratic professionals, Matthews has marveled at Reagan, whom Matthews considered in some ways the perfect political force—a President who goes home to a ranch, but also a President you can not imagine playing golf. (Yes, Reagan has played, but you know what Matthews means.) In the summer of 1986, when some silly Republicans began spilling over with idle chatter about repealing the Twenty-second Amendment that limits a President to two terms, Matthews detected something that pleased him. Reagan, Matthews thought, was having a debilitating effect on the Republican party.

Reagan, says Matthews, has been a party man in a way that Eisenhower, the last Republican to serve two terms, was not. Eisenhower was invited by representatives of both parties to seek the presidency. He decided to do so, decided to be a Republican, became President, did reasonably well, and departed in 1960 with the Republican party less strong in Congress than it was when he ran in 1952. In contrast, Reagan was, from the first, a foul-weather friend of the Republican party. A Democrat until well into middle age, he clambered aboard the Republican ship when many others were scrambling to get off—during the Goldwater campaign. Reagan was, from the start, a "conviction politician," working for an ideological movement before he began seeking an office. And when he was in the nation's highest office he toiled hard for the party that by then, and because of him, was thoroughly identified with him.

However—and this is where Matthews took heart in 1986 —the last time Reagan left an office after serving two terms as a chief executive (1974), he was replaced by someone very different. Reagan was replaced by the son of the man Reagan had defeated to become Governor in 1966: Jerry Brown. In 1974, as Reagan left office, California voters were fond of Reagan. Six and ten years later they voted for him for President. But in 1974 they refused to replace him with the man who had been, in effect, his Vice President (Houston I. Flournoy)—a lieutenant governor who had been loyal, trustworthy, decent, experienced and dull. Instead, they chose Jerry Brown, who certainly was not dull.

By 1986 Republicans were showing signs of a kind of nostalgia that has periodically afflicted Democrats. So strong was the Democratic party's affection for Franklin Roosevelt, the party had trouble wrenching its gaze from the past. It did not do so until Eisenhower gave Democrats two drubbings. Then in the 1960s there came Camelot—and then Kennedy nostalgia. The party again acquired a retrospective cast of mind and was never quite comfortable with Lyndon Johnson as President or with Hubert Humphrey as nominee in 1968.

By the seventh year of the Reagan presidency the strongest Republican feeling about the future was a desire to postpone it. In interpreting this as a sign of ideological sterility, Matthews speculates that Reagan might be remembered the way Churchill remembered Richard the Lion-Hearted: "His life was one magnificent parade, which, when ended, left only an empty plain." But that is too strong—much too strong. Reagan has not done all that he set out to do. But that distinguishes him not at all from any other President. However, he promised to slow inflation, slow the growth of the domestic side of government, and substantially increase defense spending. He has done all three. In hockey, three goals is a hat trick. Reagan's hat trick establishes him as one of the ten or so most effective Presidents.

As 1987 dawned, Reagan was, because of Iran and the natural attrition of governance, a somewhat lame duck. He had a weakened hold on the country's attention and Congress's deference. However, in 1989 he will again loom like a colossus over Washington—no mean trick for someone living in Los Angeles. His reach will extend through the decade beyond his departure from office. He will control the future debate and agenda more than any post-war President has done. The reason for this, paradoxically, his biggest failure: the deficit. The government, which is energized by money, is out of money. This is a result of Reagan's shrinkage of the government's revenue base. Every day of the Reagan presidency the government became another day older and deeper in debt.

Reagan has not been able to do what he refused to ask the voters for permission to do. He has not brought about a Reagan Revolution. Now, in the century of Lenin, Hitler, Mao and Castro, it is obviously nutty to speak of any result of an American election as revolutionary. But even allowing for the genial hyperbole of American politics and journalism, Reagan's consequences, although substantial, have not been as bold—as revolutionary, if you must—as those of FDR and LBJ. James Q. Wilson[5] notes that in this century there have been only two "windows of opportunity" opened wide enough to permit bold political change. Both of these windows benefitted liberals. In 1935 the catalyst was the Depression, then in its fifth year. There were large and solid Democratic majorities in both houses of Congress. And suddenly there was a Supreme Court majority, albeit slim, that was deferential to the political branches of government. FDR pounced on the opportunity and proceeded to build the foundations of the welfare state.

Exactly thirty years later, in 1965, the Congress that convened was exceptionally liberal, thanks to the Republican casualties occasioned by the candidacy of Barry Goldwater. In 1965, for the first time since 1938, there were liberal legislating majorities in both houses of Congress. In 1938 FDR's court-packing had provoked a backlash in the midterm elections. From 1939 through 1964 the coalition of Republicans and southern Democrats was able to conduct blocking operations. In 1965 Lyndon Johnson presented himself (misleadingly but understandably) as custodian of the agenda of an assassinated young President. Buoyed by an electoral landslide, Johnson began erecting the Great Society on the moral and institutional foundations provided by the New Deal.

Was a third window of opportunity thrown open by the 1980 election? Wilson argues, convincingly, that it was not:

The 1980 elections produced no special moment in American history. An incumbent President, beset with rampant inflation, high interest rates, and foreign-policy reversals, was defeated by a rival who had, in the voters' minds, the chief advantage of not being the incumbent. The Republican party captured the Senate and made gains in the House, but unlike in 1965 and 1935 these shifts produced no clear ideological majority that could form the basis of a new governing coalition. Little could happen against the opposition of Republicans and conservative Democrats, but little could be achieved by them acting alone, if for no other reason than that, on many issues, it was a divided coalition. Most important, public opinion, which supported the thrust of policy in 1935 and 1965, was not disposed to reverse that thrust in 1981. People wanted changes—lessened inflation, a stronger defense—but there was little demand for cuts in major welfare or environmental programs.[6]

That is why, as the Iran affair corroded the foundations of the era of good feeling, it was nevertheless unclear to what extent the corrosion would affect the Reagan agenda. What remained of the agenda? As 1987 began, the past was not prologue to some bold new chapter. In domestic policy, most of what had happened since September, 1981, had been a coda. The heart of the Reagan concert had been played by then, with the spending cuts and tax cuts.

Since autumn 1981, there had been on the spending side an ongoing referendum. Congress, reflecting—as it is very good at doing—the popular will, had said: "Enough, already." The public had wanted to stop domestic spending cuts and to slow defense increases, and both have been done. On the revenue side there has emerged, especially since the Mondale campaign, a bipartisan commitment to "revenue neutrality" in tax changes.

By 1987 the Reagan administration was waxing wicked, according to conservatives who were struck dumb—not really, but one wished they were—by amazement. The cause of the amazement was the administration's proposal to expand Medicare to provide catastrophic health insurance for the elderly. Why was this being done? As is usual in politics, there was a swirl of factors—personal, philosophic, and political. First, there was a crucial person—Otis Bowen, who was the Governor of Indiana before he became Secretary of Health and Human Services. He is a physician whose wife died of cancer after a protracted illness. In 1987 he was sixty-nine and his mother was in a nursing home. Bowen had the passion necessary to push the issue.

Others saw the political argument. Elderly voters are diligent voters, and the children of the elderly are apt to have school- and college-aged children of their own. Their parents are vulnerable to huge medical bills. So the middle-aged middle class feels vulnerable too. The political and ethical arguments for catastrophic health insurance were mutually reinforcing. But hard-shell conservatives could not be blamed for thinking they were suffering vertigo. By early 1987 the Reagan Revolution, like most revolutions, was a wayward thing. In year seven it was emphasizing sex education (to combat AIDS) and another increment on the already substantial edifice of socialized medicine. Two cheers for waywardness: The administration was defensible on both counts.

In proposing catastrophic insurance, Reagan said, with characteristic exaggeration, that his plan would "give Americans the last full measure of security." It would not, but the fact that it would not is less noteworthy than the fact that he endorsed the ideal of government providing such security. Henceforth, his objections to congressional enrichments of his plan could concern only price, not principle. However, Reagan had never opposed the principle involved. To the recurring surprise of some of his most ardent and least observant supporters, Reagan is a "New Deal Conservative" quite reconciled to modern government's steady impulse to build a "social insurance state." In 1987 Reagan was being Reagan. His legacy will include one of the most important post–New Deal enrichments of the welfare state.

However, by 1987 Americans were being reminded, yet again, of this: The presidency is an inherently, meaning constitutionally, weak office. There is little a President can do on his own except sway the country and by doing so move Congress. Thus, the power of the presidency—unlike, say, the power of the office of the British Prime Minister armed with party discipline—varies substantially with the qualities of the occupant. And the power of a particular President can vary radically with swings in the public's perceptions of him.

Again, remember that Reagan's hold on the country's affection always rested to a remarkable degree on his reputation as a politician of clear principles clearly spoken. In the nineteenth century, an exasperated (and probably jealous) critic said: "Horatio Alger wrote the same novel 135 times and never lost his audience." In Reagan's long career he has demonstrated that in a democracy you build an audience by saying a few clear and convincing things 100,000 times. Clarity and consistency, important to any President, have been especially so to this one because those qualities, rather than a reputation for expertise, have formed an unusually large part of the foundation on which approval of him rests. That was jeopardized by the attempted appeasement of Iran, the average American's least favorite nation in the 1980s. It was this attempted appeasement that Senator Alan Simpson (R., Wyo.) said "causes the bar stools to spin out in my part of the country."

The best possible interpretation of the Iran debacle was that Reagan had failed to select satisfactory subordinates and then failed to superintend them adequately. He could usefully have borrowed a page from Napoleon who, when he was bringing the benefits of French culture to Egypt, wrote to a friend: "I am having three heads cut off here every day and carried round Cairo."[7] That spectacle inclined the natives to subordination.

The Iran affair revealed a Reagan penchant for strewing banana peels in his own path. Lt. Col. Oliver North was such a peel, as was Reagan's subsequent celebration of North as a hero.

Reagan's assessment of North was a judgment characteristic of Reagan, a man prone to measuring moral qualities by intentions rather than results. It was the judgment of a sentimentalist, an anti-political judgment, an unserious judgment. One meaning of that judgment, and of the "Oliver North is a hero" lapel buttons it gave rise to, is that some conservatives are determined to have their own "Sixties" in the Eighties.

Reagan came to prominence during, and to a significant extent because of, the eruption of extremism throughout the culture of the 1960s. Extremism on the left was rationalized by incompetent ethicists who regarded an intense inner life —"sincerity"—as a justification for willful public actions, including many actions that violated laws, manners and other forms of due process. Conservatism grew, particularly among intellectuals, in reaction against such politics. Conservatives asserted traditional concern for process as a check against excess. The Iran-contra affair involved various attempts to

evade or subvert laws, established procedures and intragov-
ernmental traditions (thin reeds, these) of civility. But this
assault on the conservative value of due process did not elicit
from the foremost conservative, the President, any conspicuous indignation.

Fish got to swim, birds got to fly, and we all got to wonder
what this means for all the candidates now rising from the
underbrush like rocketing pheasants.

The unpleasantness regarding Iran is unlikely to determine
the 1988 outcome. The rhythms of American politics are such
that elections rarely turn on episodes two years old. However,
the disarray is draining away some of the Republican party's
élan, and the cachet that until recently came with attachment
to the party. In the 1980s, more than at any time in its history,
the party is identified with one person. In Teddy Roosevelt's
era, there was a rival conservative wing of the party. In Ike's
era there was a Taft wing and an emerging Rockefeller wing.
Since 1980 the GOP slogan has been "We're all Reaganites
now." In a poll conducted in June, 1986, 54 percent of the
public identified the Republican party with Reagan. Forty-six
percent identified the Democratic party with John Kennedy.
Fewer than 10 percent identified the Democratic party with
anyone in elective office at that date.

It is impossible to know the extent to which the word "Rea-
ganite" will, by autumn, 1988, be identified, on balance, with
success or failure. Presidents usually fail, and blame is appor-
tioned between them ("no leadership"), the parties (the "decline" thereof), and "the system" (that is, the Constitution's
separation of powers). But there is nothing wrong with the
system that (in Alexander Hamilton's words) "energy in the
Executive" won't cure. And effective presidential energy
comes from ideas. Parties have lost the glue of patronage that
made machines possible, so they, too, need ideas. And there
is nothing wrong with parties that unifying, animating ideas
won't cure.

The chemistry of success in presidential politics is a volatile compound of two elements, ideas and temperaments. These elements are related in complex ways. Some temperaments are especially suited to communicating ideas, and to generating the kind of public affection that makes the public receptive to ideas.

What makes effective Presidents so rare is the fact that presidential power is a function of public affection. The power of the office varies radically—compare the presidency in July, 1980, and July, 1981. It varies with the grip the occupant of the office has on the public's affection and imagination. Reagan's grip derived in large measure from his serene understanding that politics is like baseball, not football. He conducted his high office the way Earl Weaver conducts his. When Weaver was the Aristotle of the Baltimore Orioles, he said: "This ain't a football game. We do this every day." Baseball's best teams lose about 65 times a season. It is not a game you can play with your teeth clenched.

Politics is like that. And sometime in the 1970s, Americans grew weary of a government with clenched teeth. They had had their fill of the "loneliness" and "splendid misery" and other rubbish about the presidency. Reagan has been an astonishing political force because he, like his country, has a talent for happiness.

Happiness has not always had a good press. It has not always been in vogue, particularly among the intelligentsia, which tends to consider happiness a sign of unseriousness and misunderstanding of the world. Joseph Epstein has written that growing up is often understood to be a misery, and that insecurity, angst, mid-life crises and decay are the fate of grown-ups. Therefore, "we can figure on roughly 35 to 40 minutes of enjoyment in a normal life span."[8] Epstein notes that happiness can be barely described, let alone analyzed, whereas unhappiness can be analyzed to a fare-thee-well. Besides, unhappiness implies criticism of the world. This is why intellectuals are so happy when they are miserable. Epstein wrote this in an essay titled "The Crime of a Happy Childhood."[9]

Reagan is America's last President for whom the Depression is a vivid formative experience. That experience almost seems to have made him cheerful. But, then, an affirmative response to hard times—this cannot go on; happiness is just around the corner—is American as apple pie, or even a Ritz cracker. While people were living in Hoovervilles and eating saltine crackers in soup lines, someone launched a cracker called Ritz. That was like launching an expensive magazine about business during the nation's worst business crisis—and audaciously calling the magazine "Fortune." That is, of course, what Henry Luce did.

Reagan has understood that a blend of contentment and optimism—happiness with an American itch to move on—is a practical ingredient in governance. Reagan, according to William Henry, understood that the middle class's connection with politics is now mostly emotional. Members of that class "would pay their taxes to a regime that made them feel good about the country, and themselves."[10]

As the 1988 election approaches, the Republican party does not feel as good about itself as it did in 1981, and the Democratic party is coming off a period in which it certainly has not felt good about itself. Consider, first, the Republican problems.

# REPUBLICANS

For the longest time, Republicans felt unloved. After Franklin Roosevelt and then John Kennedy, Democrats seemed to have cornered the market on cachet. Between 1933 and 1980 only two Republicans won the White House. One, Eisenhower, was only a perfunctory Republican. He could as easily have run and won as a Democrat. The other Republican winner, Nixon, was a Republican through-and-through, and was less embraced than suffered by the electorate. He won—barely—in 1968 because under the Democrats the country was at its own throat. He won in 1972 because the Democratic party went on an ideological bender that produced the nomination of George McGovern.

However, in the 1970s the Republican party began to become, if not exactly glitzy, at least mildly interesting. And by the time Ronald Reagan had blasted Carter and then Mondale, the trend spotters were hard at it, spotting trends. Republicans, they said, were on a roll and might—indeed, probably would—roll on to realignment and the status of the majority party. The spotters of that trend may have been—may still be—bang on. However, it is well to remember that intellectuals and journalists and others who postulate trends often seem to acquire an emotional stake in the immortality of their trends. As George Orwell said, intellectuals and kindred spirits tend to believe that a trend will go on forever —that if Rommel gets to Alexandria, he must get to Cairo. However, Rommel got to Alexandria but not to Cairo. People learn things, such as how to decrease the risk of Rommel (or AIDS, or lung cancer). Democrats may be slow learners but they are learners.

The Republican party is not as robust as circumstances, including Democratic mistakes, have made it seem. And now Republicans must live with the consequences of something that takes a terrible attrition in politics: success. They must live with the consequences of their thoughts, words, and deeds while in power in this decade. As a Baltimore Democrat once said, "A lot of sheep are going to come home to roost."

In 1988 each party will have a fascinating task. Democrats will try to reverse, or compensate for, a twenty-year loosening of their party's grasp on traditional constituencies. Republicans will try to attach permanently to their party many of the voters attracted twice by Reagan candidacies.

Considered as a party man, Reagan is the most important Republican since McKinley. He has changed, at least through two elections, the composition of the party by his ability to draw blue-collar and ethnic voters. What made Reagan the Republicans' best bet in 1980, and perhaps what made him President, was his ability to win blue-collar voters. He got about 47 percent of them. Republicans are understandably eager to think that what has happened—call it incipient semi-demi-re-alignment—will continue. But Republicans should remember Mark Twain telling how the Mississippi had short-ened itself several times by cutting new channels, becoming straight where it had been serpentine. He said it was a lead-pipe cinch that at the rate the river had been shortening itself, in 742 years the lower Mississippi would be just a mile and three-quarters long and Cairo, Illinois, and New Orleans would sit cheek by jowl, with a single mayor.

Of course maybe what has been going on is de-alignment. There is a profound practical difference between de-alignment—the loosening of party ties—and realignment, the development of new ties. De-alignment is today well advanced. There are two minority parties, of which the GOP is the smaller. According to Richard Wirthlin, the Republican pollster, it is too soon to say whether it will stay that way.

Wirthlin was present at, and involved in, the creation of the Reagan presidency. As the candidate's pollster, and as the pollster for the President through two terms, Wirthlin has traced the aftermath of what he still considers the watershed election of 1980. In the middle of Reagan's second term Wirthlin, a conservative Utahan, still insisted that the word "realignment" was too strong to denote what had been happening. He was prepared to say only that "Americans are more comfortable with the Republican party than they were a decade ago." But his data documents a trend which, if it continues, will, Wirthlin says, be seen as protracted, rolling realignment.

A recurring question in his surveys has concerned political "leaning." The question is: "Generally do you consider yourself to be" a Democrat or a Republican? In 1979 there was a 22-point gap favoring the Democratic party, 53–31. By 1982 the gap had shrunk to 15 points (49–34) and by 1986 to 3 points (41–38). It is unclear what, if any, lasting impact, the Iran-contra debacle will have on the basic currents of American politics. It alone is not apt to derail a rolling realignment.

Wirthlin thinks that if such a realignment is to be completed, it must pass through five stages.

The first, says Wirthlin, is widespread recognition that the Democratic agenda of the last fifty years—the use of the federal government as the economy's balance wheel; the use of

federal spending and regulation to fine-tune social justice—
is no longer attractive. Wirthlin says this stage was reached in
the late 1970s. Wirthlin is unquestionably right about that.
But by 1987 the alternative conservative vision hardly
seemed like a stark contrast. The conservative administration
was even using government power to adjust currency exchange rates to regulate trade. A negotiated, meaning managed, devaluation of the dollar is, by another name, "currency
protectionism." It is a notably aggressive use of government
power to balance the economy. Regarding the use of federal
spending to fine-tune social justice, year seven of the Reagan
presidency began with the President's endorsement of catastrophic health insurance. These facts pose problems for Republicans who understand realignment as Wirthlin does,
because he says that the second stage of realignment involves
the appearance of a person who can articulate an alternative
agenda. Wirthlin says this stage was reached in 1980 with the
Reagan candidacy. The third stage is widespread recognition
that substantial change will work and that an alternative
agenda, as well as a person, is in place. Wirthlin believes this
stage was reached with the prolonged economic expansion
that began in the middle of the Reagan years.

The fourth and fifth stages have not yet been reached. The
fourth requires actions by millions of individuals—changes
of party registration by voters hitherto registered in the Democratic party. (In 1986 3 percent of the electorate—enough to
swing a moderately close election—were registered Democrats who nevertheless considered themselves Republicans.)
The fifth stage is the institutionalizing of the rolling realignment. It is denoted by such developments as active support
for the Republican party and the achievement of Republican
majorities in state legislatures.

When the fifth stage is reached, Wirthlin says, the process
becomes self-sustaining. Of course the first rule of politics, as
of the rest of life, is: Nothing lasts. So what Wirthlin must
mean is: The process becomes self-sustaining until the day

comes—as come it must—that the new agenda is no longer new, and no longer convincing, and the process of realignment begins to roll the other way.

At the heart of such a process is always a person. In the current process, the person has been Reagan. Wirthlin agrees with Nelson Polsby, the political scientist, who says the "conversion mechanism" is a function of a leader. Wirthlin says, "I believe in political bonding, as when a duckling is born and cuddles up. It might cuddle up to a chicken or goose, but whatever it cuddles up to is his mother."[1]

Mother Reagan is not part of the Republican future. That may hasten the decline of the notion that being a Republican is like eating kiwi fruit, a trendy thing that attests to one's good taste and sense of style. It is hard not to think that there has been a herd-like element to the Republican ascendancy of the 1980s. If that has been so, the ascendancy is fragile, subject to being slowed or even reversed by some change in the social atmosphere.

Did I say herd? Have you not heard a stampede? Consider the case of Florida.

It has been called America's geologic afterthought. The rest of the mainland was old hat by the time the peninsula rose a few feet out of the ocean just 20 million years ago. But Florida has been making up for lost time and today is America's foremost laboratory of social change. It has been romanticized as "a sublimated mistress" and deromanticized as "just sand with business possibilities." Whatever it is, it is jumping. In the mid-1980s upward of 1,000 newcomers were unpacking every day. In the 1986 elections 80 percent of Florida's voters were not native Floridians. Florida voters are fickle. Since 1964 only one Senator has been re-elected from Florida, land of paper plates and disposable politicians.

Now, consider this astonishing fact. From 1980 through 1986 new party registrations in Florida favored the Republican party over the Democratic party by a thumping 13-to-1 (400,000 to 30,000) margin.

Obviously the people comprising Florida's population growth are not a perfectly representative sample of the American electorate. There are many anti-Castro Cubans who tend to be Republican. Furthermore, new Floridians include a disproportionate number of elderly people living on fixed incomes. The elderly in general, and especially those with the means to flee to Florida, are better off than the average American. They may have especially sharp anxieties about inflation, anxieties that may dispose them toward the Republican party. But that hardly explains the Florida registration figures, and certainly does not explain away reasons for Democratic anxieties.

It seems reasonable to say that Florida's registration figures reflect a trend. But it is a trend on the scale of a tidal wave. Tidal waves in nature are relatively rare. They are caused by earthquakes or other large events. Tidal waves roar along until they go smash on a beach or otherwise run out of energy. A 13-to-1 registration wave looks awfully like a social tidal wave—a fad, a phenomenon driven in part by an element of fashion: Being Republican has recently been chic.

But a sense of chic is a rickety foundation for political prosperity. And some numbers suggest that the Republicans' prosperity has not been quite what it has been cracked up to be. In 1980 Reagan's 10 percentage-point margin of victory over his Democratic opponent was impressive, but it was only the eleventh biggest margin in the twenty preceding presidential elections in this century. It was smaller than four Democratic victories (1912, 1932, 1936, 1964) and six Republican victories (1904, 1920, 1924, 1928, 1956, 1972), and Jimmy Carter was the architect of Reagan's 1980 landslide.

In November, 1980, Carter lost four out of ten of his 1976 supporters. There was one dominating fact of 1980 and it was not a national conversion to conservative ideology. It was a desire to see Carter gone. William Schneider, resident fellow at the American Enterprise Institute, writing in a volume published by AEI, says the electorate was not "convinced" about conservatism but was tolerant about it, willing to give it a chance. Schneider says every election offers a "plebiscitary choice" (a chance to say how the government is being run) and an "ideological choice" (a chance to say which candidate or party comes closest to one's ideological beliefs). Carter's campaign strategy was to emphasize the ideological choice. Reagan struggled successfully to make the election turn on the plebiscitary choice.[2] That is, Reagan won because he kept the election from being a referendum on conservative ideology.

In only one region, the Mountain West, do registered Republicans constitute a majority. It is interesting that the eight states of that region (Montana, Idaho, Wyoming, Colorado, Utah, Nevada, New Mexico, Arizona) are today the way the South used to be before it became more homogenized with the rest of the nation. That is, the Mountain West has a strong sense of identity. And it is a sense compounded, as such a sense usually is, of pride and resentment.

The people of the Mountain West are inclined to think, as Southerners once did, that they have a unique "way of life" that sets them apart from and a bit above other regions. It involves, they think, a special rugged independence and self-sufficiency. These are values natural to a region the prosperity of which was originally rooted in the entrepreneurial high spirits of extraction industries and ranching. The resentment derives, as it did in the South, from a feeling of being set upon by a federal government manipulated by "flatlanders" who think the Mountain West needs to be supervised, lest it mismanage its resources. The primary cause of the region's resentment can be expressed statistically: Nevada 85 percent, Idaho 64, Utah 61, Wyoming 50, Arizona 44, Colorado 36, New Mexico 34, Montana 30. Those are the percentages of the states' land that is owned by the federal government. (East of the Mississippi, the highest federal ownership is in New Hampshire and is just 12 percent.) The Mountain West feels not only distrusted but coveted in a most unflattering way. It thinks that the rest of the country looks at its wide open spaces and thinks: Where the deer and the antelope are not playing, let's put MX missiles and nuclear waste dumps and other things we do not want right next door.

All of which has this political importance: Registered Republicans are a majority only in the region that is least like the rest of the nation, a region stubbornly fond of the Republicans' anti-Washington theme. There is one small "region" where Republicans may reasonably wonder if they will ever be a majority. It is on the south side of Capitol Hill, where the House of Representatives is. A telling fact of the first half of the 1980s was that Republican ascendancy stopped at the House door. Democrats merrily tell a joke about God promising three world leaders that he will grant each of them one wish. Britain's Prime Minister wishes for peace in Northern Ireland. God says, "OK, but it will take until 1996." So Britain's Prime Minister weeps. Israel's Prime Minister wishes for peace in the Middle East. God says, "Fine, but it cannot be done before 2006." So Israel's Prime Minister weeps. Ronald Reagan wishes for a Republican House. So God weeps.

Since 1932 the GOP has lost twenty-five of twenty-seven House elections, losing about 60 percent of the seats overall. Republicans have won landslides in four of the last eight presidential elections, but Republican strength in the House has never been above what it was (201 seats) after the first landslide (1956). There have been fifty presidential elections, and 1984's was the worst for a winner, in this sense. Never has a presidential winner had such a small percentage (41.8 percent) of his supporters in the new House.

In 1984 one in five Reagan voters voted for a Democratic congressional candidate. In 1984 Democrats won in 191 of the 372 districts Reagan carried. They won in 40 districts where Reagan got 55 percent or more.

Why is the electorate sending such scrambled signals? Perhaps voters reflexively put sand in the gears of government on the assumption that, at any time, any branch of government, no matter where it is going, is going too far. Perhaps people think Democrats like government and hence are more congressional, meaning attentive to details. Perhaps Republicans are recruiting inadequate candidates because conservatives are reluctant to uproot themselves and go to Washington to implement the conservative principle that government is deplorable and should go away. On the other hand, perhaps we are in the early stage of political trickledown, as the rising Republican tide "rises down" from the presidency. Or perhaps. . . .

In any case, 1984 was a year for incumbents. When an incumbent President runs for re-election, the incumbent is the issue. Only three elected incumbents have been beaten in this century. One (Taft, 1912) lost because of a civil war in his party. Two (Hoover, 1932; Carter, 1980) lost because more than a year before the election they were seen to be bewildered by their failures. However, 1984 was not just an unusually good year for an incumbent President. It was paradise for incumbents of all sorts. The incumbent President rolled up 59 percent of the vote. The last two incumbents to run, Ford in 1976 and Carter in 1980, won 48 percent and 41 percent respectively, and both lost. In 1984 incumbents won in 390 of the 435 congressional districts.[3] (Only 16 incumbents were defeated.)[4]

Most Democratic incumbents ran substantially ahead of Mondale. Reagan had made Americans cheerful and cheerful people do not dash around decapitating incumbents. Because the Democratic party had more incumbents, it gained more from Reagan's era of good feeling. There was rough justice in that. The good feeling was related to the robust recovery, which owed much to the Carter appointee still running the Federal Reserve Board (Paul Volcker) and to a demand-side recovery driven by the deficit. And speaking of rough justice, consider this: Liberalism generated conservatism. The "give me" spirit of the 1960s and 1970s produced demands for government services. The satisfaction of those demands produced the high inflation and taxes that caused a "give-me" revolt demanding, "Give me relief from government!"

In 1980 the nation was ripe for what Republicans do best. It was ripe for a campaign condemning the government. A negative tone has served Republicans (and Democrats) well when out of office. In 1946, the Republican slogan "Had Enough?" helped produce gains of fifty-six House and thirteen Senate seats. Twenty years later, a Republican rookie won California's governorship using the slogan in Spanish— "Ya Basta!" (literally, Enough Already).

But by autumn, 1988, a Republican will have been at the head of the government for almost eight years. So the old-style negativism will not be a useful arrow in the Republican quiver. The Republican problem in 1988 can be put concisely. The party craves some sort of extension of what has happened during the best of the Reagan years. To some extent the electorate may feel likewise. However, the winning candidates in American elections, especially when no incumbent is running, are generally the candidates who seem to be agents of change.

It is problematic for a party to come off eight years in power and present itself as an agent of change. It must do so delicately, lest it seem to be repudiating its recent past. And Republicans are going to have problems dealing with their eventful recent past.

Consider, first, foreign policy. It is the most important subject but is of secondary importance. It is the most important subject in terms of consequence, but not as an election-turning issue.

Arthur Balfour, a politician who was perhaps philosophical to a fault, said, "Nothing matters very much, and few things matter at all." Most things in politics do not matter one-tenth as much as the participants in the controversies think at the time. But foreign policy matters very much indeed. As has been said (by Harry Truman, I think), domestic policy can hurt you but foreign policy can kill you. He did not mean it can kill you politically; he meant it can literally kill you. However, elections rarely are decided by foreign policy considerations. Even in 1968, when the United States was fighting a ground war of attrition on the mainland of Asia with a conscript army using dubious tactics for an ill-defined purpose—not even then was foreign policy the issue that controlled most voters' decisions. (And of course to the extent that foreign policy was a controlling factor, it hardly produced a "peace vote." Again, the combined Nixon-Wallace vote was 57 percent.)

Furthermore, it is hard to make foreign policy as intellectually interesting as domestic policy inherently is. Library shelves groan, as do undergraduates, beneath the weight of classics of political philosophy. Not one of those is about international relations. The philosophically interesting dilemmas of social life concern people living in community, under a common sovereignty, dealing with the concepts of rights, justice, consent, representation, obligation, and so on. Writings about international relations tend either to be called forth by particular events, and to be as perishable as their contexts, or to be highly general prudential maxims. Gary Hart was, therefore, undertaking something difficult in 1986, when he delivered three lectures on "a foreign policy framework for the twenty-first century." Imagine how a "framework for the twentieth century," written in 1886, would have read fifty years later: "As regards relations between the Czarist and Hapsburg regimes. . . ."

Hart had a hand in handing the foreign policy issue to the Republicans a decade and a half ago. Hart was McGovern's campaign manager in 1972, the year the Democratic party nominated McGovern and thereby repudiated its honorable record in the post-war world. From the birth of totalitarianism in 1917, when Woodrow Wilson became its active enemy, through FDR's leadership against Europe's dictators, through Truman's response to the Berlin blockade, the threat to

Greece, and the Korean War, through Kennedy's and Johnson's commitment of U.S. power against communism in Indochina—through all that, the Democratic party was the world's foremost foe of totalitarianism. Its record of constancy was superior to that of the GOP. Then came the 1972 capture of the Democratic party by people who considered the party's post–World War II record dishonorable and discredited by the party's role as architect of the Vietnam intervention.

McGovern was an isolationist. Of course isolationism is a sin that dare not speak its name, so today it comes cloaked in the language of multilateralism. A reluctance to act other than in concert with allies achieves the traditional goal of isolationism: It immobilizes America, by making America hostage to the most hesitant member of the alliance. Today isolationism is a policy of passivity, not solitariness.

In the early 1970s, the public rhetoric—including the Republican administration's rhetoric—was soggy with detente.

Nixon overflowed about the "end of the Cold War," "an era of negotiation, not confrontation," accords on "principles of conduct." Such stuff subverted public support for diplomatic and defense measures arduous enough to prevent detente from becoming what it became: a recipe for American retreat and an incitement to Russian expansion.

It is unclear what Jimmy Carter's foreign policy beliefs were when he came to power. Perhaps they were unformed. That seems a reasonable conclusion about a man who reached late middle age in the last quarter of the twentieth century and was shocked that the Soviet Union would invade Afghanistan. Carter was perhaps less supported than immobilized by the different advice coming from his Secretary of State, Cyrus Vance, and his National Security Advisor, Zbigniew Brzezinski. The result was a public perception of weakness.

In 1980 Republicans promised abrupt, even radical departures from the pattern of McGovernite isolationism and Carterite weakness. However, as the Reagan presidency draws to a close, it is apparent that not nearly as much change has been delivered as was promised.

In the administration's foreign policy there has been a streak of unseriousness that will cripple conservative attempts to portray future presidential elections as the last two were portrayed—as stark, historic, life-and-death choices. By the summer of 1986 the administration had agreed to subsidize grain sales to the Soviet Union. So American taxpayers paid to enable the invaders of Afghanistan to buy grain cheaper than Americans could. Why? Because twenty-two of the thirty-four Senate seats contested in 1986 were in farm states. Bob Dole is Senator from the breadbasket of the Soviet Union, a.k.a. Kansas. He rationalized this Republican administration's folly by recalling Eisenhower's statement that we should sell the Soviets anything they cannot shoot back at us. Alas, bad ideas, unlike good wine, do not improve with age.

Conservatives correctly say the Soviet regime is uniquely dangerous precisely because it takes seriously its ideology of inevitable conflict with and ultimate victory over the capitalist world. But, notes Senator Patrick Moynihan, Reagan's rhetorically conservative administration is confirming one of the few tattered prophecies that still sustain Soviet ideology— Lenin's prophecy that capitalist nations would compete to dump their surpluses (turbines, locomotives, wheat) on the motherland of communism.

A serious conservative administration would have tried to dispel the superstition of arms control. No nation's security has ever been guaranteed or even significantly enhanced by arms control. After nineteen years of the arms-control "process," all evidence is that the only Soviet aims are to use the process to disrupt U.S. deployments and channel arms competition in directions disadvantageous to the United States. Yet in 1986 the administration sleepwalked into talks on a comprehensive nuclear test ban. These talks will build pressure here and abroad for a treaty inimical to U.S. interests, which require tests to check the reliability and improve the quality and security of weapons. Furthermore, at the moment when this is being written (June, 1987) it seems probable that there will soon be an agreement that will eliminate a class of intermediate range missiles from Europe, thereby enhancing the Soviet advantage in conventional forces.

Having talked well and often of the implacable Soviet challenge, of Soviet complicity in terrorism, and of dealing with Cuban adventurism "at the source," the administration has defined the tasks by which it shall be judged. Yet it has seemed to forget that its foreign policy mandate was not to improve relations between the United States and Kansas.

Historians may conclude that it was during this administration that the United States conclusively lost the Cold War. By "lost" I mean forfeited the last chance to embody in action correct thinking about the Soviet threat. This severe judgment may be justified in spite of the fact—actually, because of the fact—that this administration is wiser than its recent predecessors and probably wiser than most of its successors will be. It is the wisest the nation has had in a generation. Measured that way, it is commendable. Measured against the task, it is unsatisfactory.

This conclusion is compelled by things done and left undone, from the failure to use the weapon of enforced default against the Polish regime's debts, to the squandering of energy on the barren charade of arms control. The debacle of policy toward Poland was particularly illustrative. Poland, like all East Bloc countries and more than most of them, was subsisting parasitically off Western capital. Its lines of credit with Western banks and Western governments were life support systems. When the Warsaw regime imposed martial law, the Reagan administration had at hand a potential policy of immense leverage—the ability to stop the flow of new credits and to call the old loans. The administration refused to do so, thereby demonstrating the degree to which a conservative administration, especially, is incapable of subordinating commerce to geopolitics. The Carteresque elevation of arms control to the rank of centerpiece in U.S.-Soviet relations demonstrated the degree to which democracies allow their wishes to control their thoughts.

It once was thought that democracies could not maintain continuity in foreign policy. The American democracy has the opposite problem. Foreign policy does not trickle down from the highest levels; it rises through the bureaucracy, which defines options, narrows choices and makes continuity hard to escape. Reagan did not escape it. And he did not escape the pandemic disease of wishful thinking about the Soviet Union.

A theme of this book is that politicians' words—the most public acts of public people—matter and should be taken seriously by serious students of politics. But this does not mean that words are invariably reliable indices of a politician's probable behavior. The point is not that (in Talleyrand's phrase) politicians use words to conceal their thoughts. Rather, the problem is that words, especially those spoken in campaigns, often express values and intentions out of the context of responsibility. This does not make the words unimportant. But it does mean that words must be examined in the cold white light of the expectation that between words and deeds fall the shadows of compromises. The compromises are imposed by the recalcitrance of reality. Most politicians mean pretty much what they say and say pretty much what they mean. The gap between the way they speak and the way they later act should not automatically be called a "credibility gap." The gap usually is not a reason for cynicism; it is not evidence that the politician is untruthful or not serious. The problem is just that words, although important, often are not the last word in politics. Conditions often speak last and loudest.

That said, this can be said. If one judges Reagan's thoughts not by his words but by his follow-through in actions—if one adheres to the old axiom that you watch a politician's feet, not his mouth—then one must conclude that Reagan's thinking has been much less radical than his rhetoric. He has talked a ferocious game. He has called the Soviet Union an "evil empire," thereby bringing down upon his head a torrent of abuse. (It has come from people who it would be entertaining to hear explaining their complaint, either in terms of the Soviet Union not being an empire or the empire not being evil.) He called the Soviet Union "the focus of evil in the modern world," thereby bringing down upon his head a torrent of abuse (much of it from people who think South Africa has replaced Chile—or perhaps the Marcos regime—as the focus of evil in the modern world). But when the teleprompter had cooled off and the bureaucratic machine had reheated the usual policy options, Reagan's "management style" became decisive. By the late 1980s the phrase "management style," as applied to the Reagan presidency, had become the preferred euphemism for "passivity." And "passivity" was a minced word. The unminced word would have been laziness.

There were some departures from well-worn foreign policy grooves. The departures included the invasion of Grenada, support to the Nicaraguan contras, the bombing of Libya, and a stiffening of U.S. policy regarding arms control, emphasizing real reductions in force levels rather than merely new ceilings. But the invasion of Grenada and the bombing of Libya were as quick and as close to painless as military operations can be. Support for the contras has been controversial but has not been pursued with convincing energy. The President has consistently described the stakes in stark language, and then has made small requests for aid. The size of the requests has seemed to refute the urgency of the rhetoric.

Regarding the most important matter, the Soviet Union, Reagan has been limited by the existence of a bland American consensus that he has, I think, come to share. He, like the country, has been sold a soothing theory that explains the dynamic of the Soviet state in terms of anxieties and paranoias rather than an ideologically driven pursuit of power. The sellers of the theory have been a diverse lot, ranging from the policy-makers in the permanent government to outsiders such as Suzanne Massie, the Russophile author, who caught Reagan's interest. The theory holds that the Soviet Union is what it is (armed to the teeth, waging war on its population, and aggressive at every turn) because it has had a hard history and has not had democracy to teach it civility. This interpretation of the central drama of the century—the struggle between democracy and totalitarianism—is of almost antic superficiality, but it plays to two perennial American weaknesses, parochialism and vanity.

Intellectual parochialism causes Americans to believe that everyone is like us, or can be made to be like us, by us. Americans do not take ideology seriously, so neither do the Soviet leaders, "really." The Reagan administration has believed that Gorbachev wants to end the arms race so he can raise his people's standard of living. The administration has believed this for no better reason than that American politicians are primarily concerned with living standards. The administration has partaken of the national vanity of believing that if Soviet leaders just see our supermarkets and swimming pools, they will see the folly of trying to win an arms race with a nation this rich. (Never mind that Soviet leaders know that the crucial and less impressive variable is Congress's willingness to compete with Soviet military spending.)

The administration has believed the impediment to Soviet reasonableness is Soviet neurosis. A therapeutic U.S. policy can dispel that, especially a policy advocated by a great communicator, especially one who knows Communists from the experience of labor-union strife in Hollywood forty years ago.

Reagan has been an elemental political force because he is utterly at one with his countrymen. He is pure American, to the center of all his cells. But that means he is inclined to indiscriminate optimism. In foreign policy, such optimism produces a reluctance, even an inability, to understand that problems will *not* be dissolved by better communication, that the Cold War is *not* just a misunderstanding, that all human beings are *not* basically alike.

Perhaps Republicans think everyone is, deep down, a Republican: Everyone thinks like a banker, or a tractor dealer, or an aluminum-siding salesman. Economic motives are primary, economic calculations control everyone, everywhere. But as has been said, if Castro were governed by economic motives, he would be a banker in Havana. However, the real Castro would die of boredom running a Caribbean Sweden. Perhaps Republicans do not really think that everyone is, deep down, a Republican. But every Republican is a Republican. Many of them are businessmen, economists and lawyers, steeped in the assumptions, mores, and rationalism of their profession. Irving Kristol argues that most economists, businessmen, and lawyers are ill-suited to diplomacy. Economists think in terms of rational behavior models. But in international relations, cost-benefit analyses often are difficult, and such calculations often are rendered irrelevant by animal spirits, national atavisms, and ideological fevers. Businessmen imagine that they live in a world of ordered, regulated competition. Actually, the business environment of the 1980s is decidedly stimulating, being richly endowed with colorful characters, such as insider-traders, and exciting events, such as leveraged buyouts and other frenzies of acquisition. Nevertheless, businessmen still imagine that they live in a sphere of sober rationality. Nations do not. For lawyers, a negotiated outcome is normally presupposed, and winning is measured in adjustments at the margins of a dispute. Relations between superpower adversaries are not so mild. A capitalist country, where one person's gain can also profit another, is apt to underestimate the extent to which the game of nations is a zero-sum game, where one nation's gain is an adversary's symmetrical loss. These characteristic American attitudes may appear in especially concentrated forms in Republican administrations.

Furthermore, there is today a curious convergence between detentists and some antidetentists: Both groups think the Soviet system can be transformed by U.S. actions. Detentists speak of a restraining web of agreements. Some antidetentists ascribe Soviet dangerousness to the Soviet's ideological élan, and talk of puncturing that élan with sharp rhetoric. To the extent that Reagan believes this—and Anthony Dolan, the speech writer who authored the "evil empire" and "focus of evil" language, does believe it—his words are not at odds with his deeds, in this sense: He thinks his words are utterly serious deeds. But the Soviet system is not as malleable as the detentists think, or as rickety as some antidetentists think.

Both groups express an American inclination to believe that U.S. policy can bring about the end of the arduous and dangerous competitive relationship. A more reasonable belief is that the fundamental task of U.S. statecraft is to limit Soviet options, not change the Soviet system. It is true that the Soviet crisis is a crisis of structure, while the West's crisis is one of political will, which is more remediable. But the record of the Reagan administration hardly encourages the belief that the West's shortcomings can be easily or lastingly remedied. The Reagan administration has accepted the centrality of arms control in U.S.-Soviet relations. Therefore the only fundamental difference between Reagan and his Democratic critics concerns aid to the contras. (Democrats support aid to the Afghan resistance, although Afghanistan is not in America's backyard, and the Afghan resistance fights more ruthlessly than the contras and aims to establish a theocracy.) The stark political fact is this: One consequence of the Reagan administration is a sense of convergence between the two political parties on the subject of foreign policy. Therefore the Republican party has less of an issue to use to enkindle its most ardent activists. And regarding domestic policy the Republican party may be even more disarmed.

• • •

When some Homer comes to write an epic poem about the intellectual odyssey of American conservatism, he will want to dwell on an episode in Sydney, Ohio, in autumn, 1984. There, President Reagan, custodian of conservatism, speaking from the rear platform of a train, said: "My opponent, Mr. Mondale, offers a future of pessimism, fear, and limits. . . ."

It is enough to curl your hair: Mondale, that cad, was going around scaring the children with the thought that there are limits.

Time was when conservatism's proudest boast was a flinty realism. It looked life in the face without flinching from the facts about the costs of things. No more.

Mondale was somewhat shaky on the subject of limits. Promising more "compassion" for the poor and for lots of other folks and promising to trim the deficit at the same time, Mondale sounded like the will that François Rabelais left when he died in 1533: "I have nothing. I owe much. I leave the rest to the poor." But conservatives are supposed to be different.

Can conservatives still claim to be the realists? Well, yes, they can claim to their hearts' content. But who will believe them? Republicans have not been allowing their sense of probability to inhibit their enjoyment of fantasy. When someone asked Max Beerbohm if a particular person ever told the truth, Beerbohm said: "Occasionally. When his invention flags." That is how Republicans have behaved about the question of taxes—the little matter of paying the government's bills. Republicans scamper like cats on hot bricks from one subject (New Federalism or tax reform) to another (line-item vetos, constitutional amendments for this or that) to avoid the subject of the deficit.

Only the courtesy I learned at my father's knee keeps me from hooting when Republicans devise euphemisms, like "loophole-closing revenue enhancements," to avoid saying "tax increases." Conservatives dissolve in admiration for this insight: "There is no free lunch." It means: Someone must pay for anything that has costs. That, although hardly a sunburst, is true enough. So is this: Government—or so conservatives not long ago professed to believe—should tax sufficiently to pay for its services. For decades, conservative after-dinner speakers convulsed audiences with this thigh-slapper: "We're not getting all the government we're paying for—thank God!" But in the 1980s, a conservative administration has been cheerily telling the country that it need not pay for all the government it is getting. For every dollar of government, the Reagan administration has asked only seventy-eight cents in taxes.

Republicans have come to think that the world is their oyster and the promise of low taxes is their oyster fork. Perhaps Republicans should be marched, one by one, down to 1111 Constitution Avenue in Washington, to the Internal Revenue Service building. Carved on that building are Oliver Wendell Holmes's words: "Taxes are what we pay for a civilized society." Unquestionably, he was right. Unfortunately, the subject of taxation annihilates many Republicans' power of thought. They will not accept this: Given the fact that large additional spending cuts are politically unlikely, the country cannot pay its bills with the revenue structure that remained after the helter-skelter tax cutting of 1981.

A literary critic said it would take twelve years to undo the damage caused by Housman's lectures on poetry. It will take a lot longer than that to undo the damage caused by the public borrowing made necessary by the inability to achieve spending cuts commensurate with the tax cuts. Yet fire-eating "conservatives" who differ with those of us who think taxes must be raised denounce us as "traditional" Republicans. Times are truly out of joint when the adjective "traditional" becomes, in the name of conservatism, an epithet. Traditional Republicans believe that the public must pay in taxes for the public-services component of its standard of living. Critics of "traditional" Republicans call themselves "real" Republicans. They say the Republican party misled the country for years by stressing the dangers of deficits.

The "new" or "real" Republicans often call themselves supply-siders. Their argument is, at a certain level of generality, indisputable, but jejune. It is that there are circumstances in which increasing taxes will decrease revenues (by suppressing economic activity), and that in other circumstances a tax cut will be so swiftly stimulative that reduced rates will generate increased revenues.

But government is an adventure in particularities, not generalities. The supply-side wager (Reagan bet the currency on it) is that cuts of the size and shape enacted in 1981, in the circumstances then obtaining, have put the country on a growth path that will, combined with spending restraint, produce approximate equilibrium between spending and revenues. In pristine form, the supply-side argument combines an untoppable promise (a self-financing tax cut) with an ironclad alibi if the promise does not pan out (always blame the Fed first). If tax cuts are followed by exploding deficits, the Federal Reserve Board can be blamed for not producing a "sufficient" expansion of the money supply. Sufficiency is, by definition, whatever "permits" growth sufficient to eliminate deficits.

In 1980 Reagan ran a relentlessly "blue skies" campaign based on the supply-side premise. But the instant the election was over he embraced a gray-skies memo from two Congressmen, Jack Kemp and David Stockman. They said the nation was on the verge of an "economic Dunkirk." That was a puzzling phrase: Dunkirk was an evacuation. Who was going to put what in a boat and sail away from what? Never mind. By December 1980, the embryonic administration was stressing spending cuts. But Reagan did not shrink government. He rearranged it, moving resources toward defense.

However, the fastest growing component of the budget is not defense, which by 1986 was actually shrinking in real terms. The fastest growing component is interest on the debt.

By the end of the decade, debt service will require a sum equivalent to nearly half of all personal income-tax revenues. Most of those revenues are deducted from the paychecks of Americans who work for wages. Who receives the interest payments the government pays? American and foreign owners of capital, who have lent their capital to government by buying bonds. So, says Senator Pat Moynihan, Reagan's deficits require people who work for wages to pay vast sums to people in places like Grosse Pointe and Riyadh who rent capital to the government.

Some Republicans now think the tax reform of the mid-1980s will stimulate growth, indeed will institutionalize permanent rapid growth, because that is the way the world works, assuming that God was reading the right economics text when He designed the world. Republicans are almost certainly right that the economy should work best when government works least at influencing the flow of forces, using a finely tuned tax code. But Republicans cannot seem to get the hang of sensible rhetoric about the relationship between government and the economy. Many Republicans deplore "people who view the tax as a means of advancing changes in our social structure." Those words were in a speech delivered by a private citizen, in 1964, in support of Barry Goldwater. Ronald Reagan has gone on saying that. In 1981 he said the tax power "must not be used to regulate the economy or bring about social change." He went on saying it as he praised a tax plan that includes tuition tax credits to improve the educational system, special tax treatment to businesses, provisions to nurture energy supplies, increased personal exemptions justified as "family policy," and so on. But let social goals influence tax policy? Heaven forfend.

In fact the Reagan administration has had, as any serious administration must have, its own plan for intervention in the management of the economy. But notice this. I have just used three words—"plan" and "intervention" and "management" —that set on edge the teeth of conservatives who cut their ideological teeth reading Friedrich von Hayek and Milton Friedman. Those economists and others like them convinced a generation of conservatives that American conservatism should be identified with, perhaps even defined as, a commitment to *laissez-faire* economics.

However, the Reagan years have been years of a blurring that clarifies. The blurring of the line that separates liberal economic "activists" from conservative . . . what? Inactivists? The clarification is this: The serious argument is about the correct political ends of economic management, not the wisdom of attempting management. It is about time that became clear.

In late winter, 1933, politics became national in a new sense: Government acknowledged what conditions taught, that our lives are woven together by an industrial economy. Beginning then, the urgent question—still an open question —has been: Can a people devoted to the widest possible scope for self-interestedness—a nation of aggressive individualism—think and act collectively as much as is required to secure the public interests? The New Deal was the first event since the Constitutional Convention of 1787 fundamentally to alter the relation of the citizen to the government. The government became a powerful engine of distributive justice, influencing the allocation of wealth and opportunity, not least by underwriting the rights of organized labor.

In 1933, Congress created the Tennessee Valley Authority to operate a power plant at Muscle Shoals, Alabama. Today, urban Americans, whose idea of the pastoral is Central Park, cannot imagine the increase of American happiness wrought by rural electrification. In 1933, one in four Americans was working the land, and the land was blowing in the wind. But reclamation, irrigation, research—all sustained by government—turned agriculture into the most successful sector of American society in the subsequent half-century. The bounty of California's Central Valley is a tribute to government's, as well as nature's, creativity.

It is perverse: After fifty years in which government has cushioned so many of life's sharp edges, it has fallen in esteem. A good shoe may be one you do not notice, but that is not true of good government. The accommodations required for an ameliorative state—the cost of public claims on private productivity—became the organizing questions of our domestic debate in 1933 and remain so in the late 1980s.

That is why in the early 1980s a specter was haunting some Republicans, the specter of an economist born the year Marx died (1883). At the age of four he was puzzling about interest rates. He became one of the century's most glittering intellects. More conservatives denounce Keynes than read him, but their complaint against him is clear. It is that Keynes supplied the rationale for overconfident government "intervening" in the economy. He did so by arguing that government can fine-tune the economy by managing aggregate demand, thereby moderating economic cycles.

Some Republicans were, I'll wager, less scandalized by Nixon's crime wave than they were by his statement in 1971 that "now I am a Keynesian." In the late 1930s Keynes's thinking became a kernel of a larger ideology favoring ambitious government action to regulate society generally, for efficiency and equity. But concerning the economy, we are all "interventionists" now.

Merely by having fiscal and monetary policies and a budget, government has a profound effect on economic life. To choose certain policies rather than others, and to spend $750 billion in certain ways rather than other ways, is to choose to shape the economy in certain ways rather than others. The one choice no government has, least of all a welfare state in a developed democracy, is non-intervention. Indeed, the word "intervention" suggests, zanily, that the state exists somehow outside the economy, rather than being woven into its fabric. The public sector is, after all, a sector of the economy.

Keynes and his disciples in the New Deal favored using

"pump priming" government spending to manage demands. He wrote:

> If the Treasury were to fill old bottles with bank notes, bury them at suitable depths in disused coal mines which are then filled up to the surface with town rubbish, and leave it to private enterprise on well-tried principles of *laissez-faire* to dig the notes up again . . . there need be no more unemployment, and with the help of the repercussions, the real income of the community would probably become a good deal larger than it is. It would, indeed, be more sensible to build houses and the like; but if there are practical difficulties in the way of doing this, the above would be better than nothing.[5]

In practice, if not in theory, Republicans do not recoil in horror from the notion of large public works. The biggest public-works project in U.S. history was launched by a conservative Republican President, Eisenhower. (Perhaps no one thought that anomalous, because the interstate highway system concerned a core American value—cars—and thus was beyond ideology.) However, in the late 1970s an economic theory uncongenial to public spending—the supply-side rationale for low marginal tax rates—came to be considered an intensely practical instrument of politics.

This is an odd time for economic theory to underpin a political strategy. In medicine, when many remedies are suggested, that often means the disease cannot yet be cured. In economics, multiplying prescriptions for achieving low inflation and low interest rates and low deficits mean we do not know how to achieve these goals simultaneously. Yet many restless Republicans have nailed their flag firmly to the mast of economic science. It is science that is, shall we say, leavened by the common political tendency to allow wishes to become the fathers of thoughts. Politics often is the art of imaginative assuming. The Great Assumption of the early

1980s was that the moment was ripe for a self-financing tax cut. The unspoken Second Great Assumption was: Well, o.k., suppose it doesn't work—suppose the tax cut is not self-financing. In that case we can win budget cuts sufficient to compensate for whatever reserves the tax cuts fail to stimulate.

In the late 1980s, many Republicans must be suffering intellectual dizziness. For years the GOP was impervious to untested new ideas. It also was impervious to tested old ideas, but about 97 percent of all ideas are false, so there was something to be said for a party that had nothing to do with any of them. Republicans, unlike those flighty Democrats, could not be swept off their feet by assistant professors. But by the late 1970s Democrats were running everything in Washington and time was hanging heavy on Republican hands. Those hands began picking up books and learned journals. Suddenly, wherever two or more Republicans were gathered, there you would hear Gilderisms intersecting Laffer curves.

The supply-side approach to tax cutting fit a political need. Many Republicans, exemplified by Representative Kemp, believe the Republican party became the "party of pain," of "root canal politics," of grim virtues like balanced budgets achieved through austerity in the domestic agenda. Supply-side economics turns on the promise of self-financing tax cuts —cuts that so stimulate economic activity that lower rates generate higher revenues and allow conservative financing of the post–New Deal state.

The swift rise of the supply-side idea in Republican circles reflects a phenomenon noted by James Q. Wilson of UCLA. The political system has become so open to ideas generated by elites that changes of public policy are increasingly often the result not of changes of public opinion but of changes in the way political elites think. But look at what was going on in the mind of the Reagan administration by 1987. The technical term, says Pat Moynihan, is "cognitive dissonance."

That is psychological conflict resulting from the strain of believing starkly incompatible ideas. Two such are that the administration's defense program is good and the administration's taxophobia is good. Cognitive dissonance can produce first passivity, then fury, hysteria, fantasizing and denial. That, gentle reader, is a description of your government at work regarding budgeting and the deficit.

In 1980 the conservative critique of liberalism boiled down to this essence: Liberalism has lost the capacity to establish rational priorities and make hard choices. Less than six years later that has a hollow ring. And so does that hoary old element of Republican rhetoric, Congress-bashing. Another casualty of the Reagan years is the Republicans' ability to blame Congress for runaway federal spending.

It is said we owe to the Middle Ages humanity's two most destructive inventions—gunpowder and romantic love. But let this be said for the Middle Ages: People understood government. They especially understood that kings (read: Presidents), not parliaments (read: Congress), are the principal impediments to reasonable public finance. Kings were constantly siphoning off the nation's wealth to build palaces, or liberate Jerusalem, or, even more peculiarly, to explore what was to become Florida. Parliaments tried to pull the purse strings.

After 500 years of enlightenment, there is less understanding. Americans think Congress is the big deficit-maker. Never mind Lyndon Johnson's guns-and-butter choice, and never mind Ronald Reagan's guns-and-tax-cuts choice. And never mind that while Reagan has been presiding over the production of more than half of this nation's federal debt, he has not found much to veto on budgeting grounds. This is because Congress has spent about what he has requested. And Congress has enacted only as many balanced budgets as he has submitted.

Of course, Presidents veto for other than budgetary reasons.

Still, it is indicative that FDR averaged fifty-seven vetoes a year, Eisenhower twenty-three, and Reagan, in his first term, only ten a year.

Now comes naughty Norman Ornstein to use history to rehabilitate Congress' reputation. Someone should silence him before he spoils the sport of Congress-bashing. He demonstrates that congressional irresponsibility has not been the primary cause of the many deficits that have produced our national debt.

In an essay for the American Enterprise Institute, he notes that the $80 million Revolutionary War debt was cut nearly in half by 1811. The War of 1812 tripled the debt, but it was almost eliminated in the 1830s. It rose as a result of the Mexican War, but then declined until the Civil War produced a $2.6 billion national debt. That caused Congress to centralize spending. A result was the creation of two powerful appropriations committees.[6] In thirty years (1867–1897), there were twenty-seven surpluses. In thirteen years revenues exceeded expenditures by 25 percent.[7]

The Spanish-American War, combined with the 1896 recession, initiated 20 years with eleven deficits. Nevertheless, in 1916 the national debt was approximately what it had been in 1896. After 127 years the Republic's debt was $1.23 billion.[8] But by 1919 the foremost shaper of the modern world—modern war—had increased the debt twenty-fold, to $25.5 billion. Then Congress again tightened budget procedures and the debt again shrank, to $16 billion by 1930.

Depression deficits were almost trivial compared to those of World War II—$211 billion.[9] The national debt as a percentage of the gross national product was 33 percent on the eve of the Depression, 43 percent in 1940, 128 percent in 1946.[10] So in 1946 Congress cut the number of committees and took other measures to restrain spending. Thanks to that and economic growth, the national debt as a percentage of GNP shrank to 98 percent by 1949, 56 percent by 1961. But in the next quarter-century there was just one small surplus

($3.2 billion in 1969). From 1960 to 1980 the debt grew from $293 billion to $993 billion.[11] Then it exploded. In Reagan's first term it nearly doubled. There also was at least a doubling of the clamor against Congress and in favor of constitutional amendments to restrain Congress.

Although Congress has been, in Ornstein's words, "an accomplice,"[12] it has been less important as a deficit-maker than Presidents. To repeat, there was Lyndon Johnson with a guns-and-butter policy. And there was Reagan's gamble that the stimulative effect of his tax cuts would make the tax cuts virtually self-financing, eliminating the need for politically hazardous budget cuts hitting middle-class programs.

Ornstein acknowledges that Congress has contributed to the deficit problem by the decline of its institutional tough-mindedness and the rise of "subcommittee government" which has weakened the central control of spending through appropriations committees. And Congress has mastered the art of bestowing blessings by tax breaks rather than appropriations. But Congress has reduced politically profitable discretionary domestic spending by reducing the amount of such spending (as a percentage of the budget) and the amount of discretion (by adopting formula programs). Furthermore, in the 1970s Congress indexed entitlement programs, thereby stopping the politically advantageous but fiscally irresponsible process of voting ad hoc increases every few years.[13]

In 1982 Congress, dragging a reluctant President, attacked the deficit by raising taxes in an election year. In 1983 it attacked the deficit by initiating an energy-tax increase. In 1984 there again was something like congressional government, with another attempt to reduce the deficit by raising taxes in an election, with an essentially passive President acquiescing.

Reagan has supported almost all the water projects President Carter tried to kill, has supported "swollen farm subsidies and generous farm-loan guarantees," has supported subsidized electric power and grazing fees for his Western friends, has pledged that he will "not stand for" cuts in the biggest sector of big government (Social Security), and wants some new deficit-enlarging programs, such as tuition tax credits. "These," says Ornstein dryly, "are not the habits of a President who would wield the item-veto pen mercilessly." [14]

The proposed item veto would cover only appropriations bills, and only a small portion of spending is controlled by such bills. In the $1,093.9 billion fiscal 1987 budget there was just $801 billion in non-defense discretionary spending. Ornstein actually thinks an item veto might increase spending because Presidents would use it as a club to threaten legislators who oppose spending the President favors. For example, Ornstein says that in Reagan's hands the item veto could be used to threaten dams and federal buildings desired by legislators opposed to MX. We would wind up buying the dams and buildings—and the larger number of MXs. [15]

Ornstein, you see, is doubly insufferable to Republicans. He robs them of two comforts, the image of Congress as a convenient villain, and the hope that constitutional tinkering can be a panacea. This is not to deny that Congress, too, is culpable. However, the problem, as conservatives should by now see, is not so simple as the defeat of conservatives by free-spending liberals. In 1983, when Republicans controlled half of Congress, they gave a tidy illustration of how conservatism can bite itself on the ankle. Consider the short, unhappy life of one recent panacea—or, if you prefer, 2,478 panaceas. I refer to the report of the Grace Commission.

Peter Grace is the businessman who chaired the commission of 2,000 people from the private sector who studied cost-control in the federal government. They came up with 2,478 recommendations. Reagan seized upon those recommendations as a refutation of the Bolshevik notion that a tax increase would be required to reduce the deficit to safe proportions. He hailed the 2,478 recommendations as "ways in which government can be made more economic and efficient by simply turning to modern business practices." Well, sort of.

Perhaps Reagan had not read all of the ten-foot high stack of 2 million documents that backed up the forty-seven Grace volumes. The mundane truth was that the largest sums that would be saved or earned by these proposals did not involve correcting "waste, fraud or abuse." Rather, they would involve changing policies adopted and continued and expanded by Republican and Democratic administrations alike. If all the 2,478 recommendations had been adopted, they would have saved or earned $438 billion over three years (the years 2001 to 2003). But the largest single chunk—14 percent of the total—was to come from a single recommendation: Cut federal pensions, civilian and military.

Uh huh. Let me reveal what the reaction to that proposal was not. It was not 537 palms slapping the 537 foreheads of all the people who are in Washington because they have won elections. They did not slap their foreheads and exclaim, "Gadzooks! Why didn't we think of that?" They are not keenly interested in cutting pensions for 4.9 million federal workers and their spouses. In fact, if Reagan had acted on, or even just endorsed, the dozen or so most important of the 2,478 recommendations he characterized as "modern business practices," he would have lost fifty states in 1984. Here is a speech he might have given, but of course was too prudent to give:

My fellow Americans, so eager am I to practice what the Commission preaches, I will urge Congress to cut federal pensions. Surely the 4.9 million federal workers and their spouses will hold Peter Grace, not Ronald Reagan, responsible. The Commission says we can save around $50 billion over three years by reducing "management overhead." That is a fancy-pants way of saying cut federal civilian employment. Praise the Lord and pass the ax: the Commission says cut hundreds of thousands of employees. True, it has taken me three years to approach my goal of reducing non-Defense civilian employees by 75,000 and during those three years civilian employment at Defense is up 83,000.

But I never subscribed to the axiom "If at first you don't succeed, destroy the evidence that you tried."

The Commission says we can save $4.97 billion over three years by repealing the Davis-Bacon Act, which raises construction wages on federal projects. Shucks, yes, I remember that in October, 1980, to counter Jimmy Carter's charges that I was anti-labor, I mailed a flier to Pennsylvania and Ohio voters pledging not to repeal Davis-Bacon. But as a wit once said, campaign promises are like New Year's resolutions, thrown together at the last moment, with little thought as to how they can be gracefully broken. Ho ho.

Now, men: Looking for a Valentine's Day present for the little lady? I am selling the Bonneville and other federal power administrations for $26 billion. (This is going to mean doubling or tripling of electricity bills for millions of users. If they want to complain, at the end of this broadcast I will give Mr. Grace's home phone number.) Look on the bright side: You can be the first on your block to own an airport. As the Commission suggests, I am selling National and Dulles—a steal at $450 million.

The Commission wants me to throw another log on the "fairness" fire by lopping lots of billions more from means-tested entitlements. And it wants me to do some enhancing, revenue-wise. For example, it says I can enhance user fees for inland waterways and related services to the tune of $3 billion. Never mind that in the last decade Congress has swatted down at least half a dozen attempts to increase fees less than half that much. Out West, where men are men and believe in me and low grazing fees, those fees are going up. So, therefore, is the price of beef, but we all eat too much red meat anyway, right?

Last but certainly not least: I love movies. Have you seen *The Year of Living Dangerously*? Well, you're about to. The Commission seems to suggest (it is almost impenetrably murky here) taxing as income all federal benefits to corporations and to individuals above a certain threshold. Today only the wealthiest 8 percent of Social Security recipients pay taxes on their benefits. The Commission has spoken, so I am going to tax most of the other 33 million— and many recipients of veterans' pensions, black lung and other disability pensions, disaster loans and other subsidized loans, farm supports, aid for dependent children . . . . I could go on but I am out of time. Good night—or perhaps goodbye.

Congress, too, used a trowel to lavish praise on the Grace Commission. Then Congress tumbled over itself in antic haste to send Reagan a bill that did the opposite of what the Commission proposed concerning federal sales of hydroelectric power. The proposal was that federal power-marketing administrations charge for their electricity something more than mere cost-recovery rates, if not the full rate the market would bear. Congress, and especially congressional conservatives; soon had a chance to stop praising and start implementing the Grace recommendations with respect to the Hoover Dam.

Since 1937 the dam has been generating electricity under a contract that guaranteed cheap power to parts of Nevada, Arizona, and Southern California for fifty years. In 1984 the contract still had three years to run. Congress then as now had so much work and so little time that it could not pass even appropriation bills in a timely manner. The Depression-era Hoover rates are from one-fourth to one-fourteenth those that unsubsidized Americans pay. Nevertheless, Congress rushed to extend for thirty years, until 2017, the cheap sale of this federal resource.[16]

The vote in the Republican-controlled Senate was 64 to 34, with every Senator from west of Missouri voting to continue the subsidy. That is Reagan country, pardner. Out where the deer and the antelope have to watch where they roam lest they bump into gun-toting, rock-ribbed, hairy-chested, Goldwaterite, sagebrush-rebellion, government-hating conservatives. But it is also where there are other cheap federal power arrangements.

Furthermore, conservative cowboys can spot trouble coming across a far mesa. They saw a slew of troubles in the suggestion that federal resources should be sold at something approaching market rates. Suppose that obnoxious principle were applied to water or grazing fees on public lands. Those folks whose church-going clothes include cowboy boots and Adam Smith neckties worship at the altar of the GFM (Glorious Free Market). But this was hitting close to home.

Conservative Republican Senators said (hang on tight— this argument can give you ideological whiplash) it would be *"laissez-faire* economics—the public be damned" to end federally subsidized rates. They said it is good, conservative government-bashing policy to continue this subsidy. Why? Because it is "consumer protection" to prevent big government from charging big (market) rates. Anyway, they said, it is sound antigovernment policy to prevent government from going "into business to make a profit." (What happened to Reagan's sound business practices? Hush.) Besides, subsidized power is—stand up and salute, conservatives—a "tradition."

As Mark Twain said, get the facts first—you can distort them later. The fact is that the Congress again demonstrated the real conservatism of modern government, which labors to protect people from disagreeable change. Twain also said that thunder is impressive, but lightning does the work. The Grace report was thunderous, but Congress would not do the work.

The Reagan years—the *soi-disant* "conservative era"— have underscored something for, and about, Republicans. They must now acknowledge that at any time, no matter which party is in control of which chamber, what Congress does is market research. Congress finds out what people want and tries to deliver it. The people want a lot, as Senator Fritz Hollings of South Carolina explains with characteristic pungency. Most speeches by Senators strike me the way a violin solo struck Bertie Wooster: "It was loud in spots and less loud in other spots, and it had that quality which I have noticed in all violin solos, of seeming to last much longer than it actually did." [17] But Hollings's speeches have snap, crackle, and pop. Consider the one Hollings uses to dramatize the dichotomy in the public's mind:

> A veteran came back from the Korean War and went to college on the GI Bill; bought his house with an FHA loan; saw his kids born in a VA hospital; started a hardware business with SBA loans and advice; got his electricity from TVA and, later, his water from an EPA project. His parents retired to a farm on Social Security, a farm on which they got their electricity from REA and their soil testing through USDA. When his father became very ill, the family was saved from financial disaster by Medicare and a life was saved with a drug developed through NIH research. His kids participated in the school lunch program, learned physics and math in high school from teachers retrained in an NSF program, and were able to go to college through the guaranteed student loans. He drove his car to work every day on the Interstate and moored his boat in a channel dredged by the Army corps of engineers. When floods hit his town, a couple of years back, he took Amtrak up to Washington to apply for disaster relief, and, awaiting his meeting, he spent part of his day visiting the Smithsonian museums and the Washington Monument.
>
> And then—after all that was said and done—he sat down one day and wrote his Congressman an angry letter asking the federal government to get off his back, and he complained about paying taxes for all those programs created for ungrateful people who were getting a free ride. [18]

This is a decade when Americans must do a lot of growing up, so someone must talk to them just like that. The government we have did not come about overnight, or by accident or conspiracy. Middle-class Americans who are the articulate complainers about it are the principal benefiters from it. They have no intention of dismantling it, so they had better pipe down and pay up.

"The difference between Ronald Reagan and Fritz Hollings," says the latter, "is that Ronald Reagan hates government." That is a bit strong, but Hollings has a point. Today's Republicans are better at praising values than they are at seeing how to use government to nurture those values. Hence it sometimes seems that the Republicans' only sincerely held value is hostility to government. And Republicans look like startled innocents when they wake up to the fact that their corrosive anti-government rhetoric has made it hard to persuade the country to trust the government with an additional $1.6 trillion for defense.

Republicans must campaign in 1988 in the shadow cast by eight years of experiences that have shown that the political rhetoric praising small government is "a kind of civic religion, avowed but not constraining."[19] Pat Moynihan uses those words to describe FDR's 1932 pledge to balance the budget. However, the description also fits the Republican party as it confronts America's fundamental choice: How much economic growth do we want, and how much government?

Since the New Deal, Republicans have argued that national policy has unduly sacrificed economic growth to the growth of government. Moynihan argues in a recent lecture that since 1981 a Republican administration has "acted in a manner that intensified the trends it most deplored." Pledged to reduce government and increase the rate of economic growth, it has been "bringing about just the opposite." Moynihan says that the paradox of Republicanism in power is this: "In effect, big government was made cheap."[20]

The growth of America's GNP was 4 percent in the 1950s and 1960s. It dropped below 3 percent in the 1970s and has been barely above 2 percent in the 1980s.[21] Since 1960, the overall increase in the U.S. manufacturing productivity of 2.7 percent a year has been less than that of nine European countries (e.g., France, 5.5 percent; Britain, 3.6 percent) and about one-third that of Japan (8.0 percent).

Now, what has happened to government recently? Between fiscal 1980 and fiscal 1986, federal outlays rose from $590.9 billion to $979.9 billion. The federal debt has soared from $914.3 billion to more than $2 trillion. In Moynihan's words, we borrowed $1 trillion from the Japanese and had a party—a party of consumption, including a flood of foreign goods.

Ronald Reagan's first presidential act, executed on Inauguration Day, was a federal-employee hiring freeze. He said it "will eventually lead to a significant reduction in the size of the federal work force." Well. At the beginning of fiscal 1981, federal employment, civilian and military, was 4,966,000. At the beginning of fiscal 1986, it was 5,210,000, with most of the increase civilian.

Why does government grow? On August 17, 1986, David Hoffman, White House correspondent for *The Washington Post,* reported that Reagan at the Illinois State Fair boasted— yes, boasted: "This year alone we'll spend more on farm support programs . . . than the total amount the last administration provided in all its four years." The farmers interrupted his eleven-minute speech with applause fifteen times. On August 13, 1986, another paper reported that Reagan told farm audiences: "No area of the budget, including defense, has grown as fast as our support of agriculture."

As Moynihan says, growth of government is a natural, inevitable product of the political bargaining process among interest groups that favor government outlays that benefit them. This process occurs under all administrations. What is different today—so different in degree that it is different in kind—is the radical discontinuity between Republican rhetoric and results. "Once through the $100 billion deficit barrier," Moynihan says, "then the $200 billion barrier; once through the $1 trillion debt barrier, then the $2 trillion barrier

—the politicians were free to soar! After all, no seeming harm had come of it." This is what Moynihan means when he says "big government was made cheap."[22] Because of the numbing deficits, the money did not seem to matter much.

There are many facets of the modern world that explain why the civic religion of small government is unconstraining. Knowledge, says Moynihan, is a form of capital, and much of it is formed because of government investment in public education. Our knowledge-based society is based on a big-government provision. Also, knowledge begets government. An "information-rich" society by its own dynamic learns about matters that make government goods and services either economically rational, as in government support for scientific agriculture, or morally mandatory, as in medicine.

Not long ago, most American workers were farmers. Today about 3 percent are, and they feed all of us and many more around the world. The most important cause of this revolution was knowledge generated and disseminated by government. The social sciences and medical science have produced knowledge that has, in turn, driven government in the direction of activism. Antipoverty programs became a moral choice only after we learned how to measure poverty. Time was, Moynihan notes, when the biggest hospital expense was clean linen. Now we have knowledge of kidney dialysis and numerous other technologies. We can choose to keep people alive, and so we do, and it costs money.

As society's wealth has increased, so have demands on government. There are limited amounts of clean air and water. But a "people of plenty" accept fewer limits than a society of scarcity. They make the collective purchase of environmental improvements. All these are tendencies of societies such as ours. Tendencies are not inevitabilities. But, Moynihan warns, a society that refuses to recognize its tendencies intensifies them. So does a political administration that will not recognize limits, including political limits.

Reagan is inexplicably fond of—he is constantly quoting—

that stupendously dumb statement by Tom Paine: "We have it in our power to begin the world over again." Oh no we don't. Paine's statement is the most unconservative statement that ever issued from human lips. Conservatism is grounded in an appreciation of the immense, constraining givenness of life. Conservatism is the politics of prudence, which begins with acceptance of the fact that, more often than not, and to a degree that is humbling to human beings, the inertia of society and history severely limits the pace and degree of change that human willfulness can bring about. Or, as a wise man once said: In the battle between you and the world, bet on the world.

Democrats came down with a bad case of more-in-sorrow-than-anger solemnity in 1981 when Republicans came to power and started acting up—that is, started acting to change things. The liberal argument was, as usual: Liberalism promotes change, conservatism respects tradition and precedent, so when liberals are in power they should institute whatever changes please them, and when conservatives come to power they should treat liberal precedents as hallowed traditions. Conservatives are not delighted with this division of political labor.

Reagan tried to devise a different division. The retired actor had not really retired when he came to Washington. He came to play the role of Tom Sawyer, who was the quintessential American, which means he was something of a sharpie. Tom, a cunning rascal, grew up about 185 miles west of Dixon, Illinois. Cunning rascals sprout like corn out there. Not since Tom tricked the other boys into whitewashing Aunt Polly's fence for him has there been anything as brazen as Reagan's plan for getting others to do his disagreeable chores. In effect he said to Congress: Here is the division of labor, I'll look after the Marine band, Air Force One and Camp David, and I'll take credit for cutting taxes. You folks cut the social programs.

The Democrats declined the honor of the role assigned

them. Conservatives were eager to start cutting, but they had problems with The Question.

In the early Seventies some conservative senators traveled to Maryland's eastern shore to plan an agenda. When returning they met the local Congressman, who asked: "What are you doing?" They said: "Saving the world." He replied by asking The Question: "Got the votes?" The world remained unsaved, and so it remains.

By 1987—indeed well before then—it was clear that the budget cutting was basically over. The 1981 budget cuts came when Reagan was at the peak of popularity, the Republican contingent in Congress was unprecedentedly united, the Democrats were bewildered and weakened by defections. The cuts passed, but it was only by the skin of the Republican elephant's tusk that the vote occurred. There would have been governmental gridlock had the Republicans not controlled the Senate. Without control, they could not even have gotten Reagan's agenda onto the Senate calendar.

"The Reagan Revolution," writes David Stockman, "as I had defined it, required a frontal assault on the American welfare state."[23] Precisely: as Stockman, not Reagan, defined it. The "revolution" was to have had two parts, the tax cut and whatever spending cuts were necessary to pay for it. Reagan got most of the former and little of the latter, creating an imbalance that was made worse by his finest achievement—the conquest of inflation. Cutting inflation was like another tax cut: The post-war growth of government was largely financed by revenue raised by "bracket creep," as inflation floated taxpayers into higher brackets.[24] All this is broadly understood now because the 1980s have been a crash course in the federal budget. There has been a rolling referendum on domestic spending. After a cold shower of facts, the country is wiser but also sadder, because it now must forgo the fun of feeling virtuous merely by generalized antigovernment thunder.

Stockman's "revolution" rested on the theory that the "will

of the people was at drastic variance with the actions of the politicians."[25] But Reagan turned out to be "a consensus politician, not an ideologue."[26] And the consensus? The voters did not vote for radical discontinuity, for a revolution against the post–New Deal role of government.

Stockman said the "dirty little secret of the Republican party"[27] is that 80 percent of House Republicans and 90 percent of Senate Republicans voted for the major expansions of the welfare state during the last thirty years.[28] Secret? Only ideological spectacles enabled Stockman to reach age thirty-four unaware of the fact that the modern state is not an accident, or a conspiracy foisted on the nation. The American people really do want mild social democracy, sacrificing some capitalist efficiency in the interest of equity and security. This fact about the sainted people is inconvenient for the large and growing number of conservatives who refer to themselves, oxymoronically, as "populist conservatives." All American radicalisms begin with deep bows toward "the people" and angry blasts at "elitism." But there is something odd about such "populism." Congressman Newt Gingrich (R., Ga.) says the government produced by twenty-five federal elections in that last fifty years represents manipulation of "the people" by a self-serving elite. What Gingrich cannot explain is why, if "the people" are such a font of wisdom and vigor, they are so thoroughly duped and tamed? Americans usually get what they want, and get rid of what they do not want, without long delays. For half a century the electorate has been electing (and usually re-electing for as long as the incumbents desire) the legislators who have woven the tapestry of federal laws that Gingrich considers foolish or worse. He must be saying that the voters have used their votes foolishly, or have desired foolish things. Is that not an elitist position? Sure it is, but there is nothing wrong with that. Leadership is inherently an act of elitism. It is the confidence of the few that they can turn the many on to better paths.

Today's government was built by both parties, in conformity with their professional readings of the desires of the middle class. It does not represent a five-decade distortion of the "real" wishes of "the people." The logic of Gingrich's radicalism is that the country has long needed leaders who could restrain the public's inclination to pile up power for the central government to use in allocating the nation's energies.

But the Republican right cannot have it both ways; it cannot have its critique of modern government and its populism, too. If this democracy is going downhill fast, the *demos*—the people—must bear a large portion of the blame. So "conservative populism" is contradictory. It is, of course, flattering to "the people" to be told that they are virtuous and that an elite is to blame for the nation's ills. But is such flattery what is needed? It certainly is not new. And it crops up in the darndest places.

In May, 1985, Treasury Secretary James Baker told an audience that tax reform is rooted in populism, which is "opposed to elitism, opposed to excessive concentrations of power and oriented toward fairness."[29] Baker's call to egalitarianism was well received by his audience, the Houston Chamber of Commerce, which peered under the table and behind the potted palms to make sure no elites were lurking.

Liberals traditionally talk as though they can pluck from thin air the indisputable truth about the "fairness" of everything. Conservatives should not compete on that field. Rather, they should earn respect by results born of realism. But "populist conservatism" is the wave of the future. Populism historically involves impatience with complexity, suspicion of big institutions and big people, and reverence for whatever "the people" are thought to believe this week. So "populist conservatism" is an oxymoron.

Decades of conservative complaining about big government have encouraged the conclusion that the country's increased conservatism reflects dissatisfaction with the gross "size" of government as measured by government's share of GNP and as exemplified by the big social-insurance entitlement programs. Conservatives, their intelligence numbed by their own rhetoric, came to the erroneous conclusion that the country was ready for large cuts in those large programs. Today's deficits are in part a monument to that misanalysis and the excessive confidence it encouraged concerning budget cutting.

The growth of government spending in recent decades has indeed been largely in the social-insurance area. But it is not the "size" of government, gauged by such spending, that has been the principal conservatizing irritant to the country. Rather, the irritant has been the increased intrusiveness of government, an intrusiveness perceived as irrational, arrogant, and bullying. Of course intrusiveness is in the eye of the beholder. One person's intrusiveness is another person's governmental vigilance on behalf of justice. But millions of Americans found intrusive and intolerable such government actions as forced busing to achieve racial balance, mandatory reverse discrimination (a.k.a. "affirmative action") including hiring and firing quotas that overrode seniority claims, the minute supervision of businesses by bureaucratic administrators of occupational safety and health regulations, the supplanting of community standards by national requirements regarding regulation of pornography, the overturning of fifty state judgments concerning the regulation of abortion, the banning of voluntary prayer in public schools, the banning of even a minute of silence in public schools (lest a pupil lapse into an unconstitutional frame of mind), judicial fine-tuning of public displays of religious symbols (the Christmas crèche on the courthouse lawn), and on and on and on. No particular intrusion offended everyone, or even a majority. But the accumulation of aggrieved minorities produced a national mood.

Of course, inflation, which was correctly understood as made in Washington, was the most conservatizing intrusion in American lives. The clearest mandate in 1980 was to reduce inflation, then known as "public enemy number one." The President arrested that public enemy. Granted, he did it with the help of Jimmy Carter's most important contribution to the nation's good: Paul Volcker. Inflation was dampened in the orthodox way, by a recession in which Volcker's Federal Reserve Board stayed the course by refusing to use money creation to soften the effect. This had wrenching effects. Unemployment rose, as did business bankruptcies. But in the late 1970s, and in the 1980 election, the public had spoken about as clearly as it ever does, and it had proclaimed that inflation was "public enemy number one." The public wanted inflation suppressed and the public got what it wanted. It was on Reagan's watch that inflation was wrung from the economy, and to Reagan goes, deservedly, the credit. It is an achievement of large, even historic proportions. It was unexpected and is, indeed, largely unexplained. Who would have guessed that falling inflation would coincide with exploding deficits?

The conquest of inflation (for the moment) is a paradigm of what will be the Republican problem after eight years in office. For Republicans, the conquest is a success with a stinger in its tail. The conquest changes a climate in which Republicans prosper.

Inflation was the great gift of history to conservatives in the 1970s. Inflation more than any other factor—more than Soviet adventurism under the cover of detente, more than Iranian hostage-takers, more than all the cumulative irritants of federal domestic policies—shoved the average American rightward. Inflation also shoved the bond market into despair, a fact that surely riveted the Fed's attention as much as public opinion did. There is almost nothing that can reasonably be called "public opinion" about the actions of the Fed. For the average American the Fed is a riddle wrapped in an incomprehensible economics textbook. Perhaps nowhere else in government is there such a wide gap between the real forces at work and the public's understanding of what is happening.

The political fact that mattered was that inflation was the comprehensive government irritant, irritating every day in many ways, in many places—at the supermarket checkout counter, the gas pump—everywhere. Inflation is an extraordinary corrosive force, sowing insecurity and resentment, both of which are sources of political volatility. Inflation is a powerful delegitimizer of governments. In fact, a wave of inflation was just what conservatives needed to surf on en route to Washington.

But once inflation is perceived to have been put back in its bottle, people find it amazingly easy to think the cork in that bottle is tapped in tight. So they turn their attention to other complaints. The difficulty of taming inflation is so soon forgotten. But while we wait for the next series of mistakes to pull the cork out of the bottle, let the record show that Reagan's foremost domestic achievement has been to demonstrate that a democracy can resist some of the internal indisciplines that fuel inflation. Reagan's resistance was not any comprehensive opposition to the fundamental political impulses of the welfare state. Rather, his resistance was narrowly but effectively confined to two negative policies. He did not opt for pump-priming spending during the depth of the recession, and he did not join in pressuring the Fed to ease up. Nevertheless, Reagan has earned considerable bragging rights. Oddly, and ideologically, he prefers to brag about other things.

Presidents should not be expected to offer a balanced assessment of their own achievements. Reagan certainly did not when, in an interview with *Fortune* magazine, he was asked whether his administration might be "just a four-year blip off the long-term national direction." He responded:

"No, I feel that we did just about a 180-degree turn in the course of government, and I'd like to feel that it reflects what the people out there are thinking."[30]

Now, leave aside the question of in what sense it can ever

be said that the people "out there" are thinking about the course of government. But it should again be emphasized that Reagan's statement, like other persons' hyperbole about a "Reagan revolution," is notably unhistorical. Nothing Reagan has done or aspires to do is comparable to what Franklin Roosevelt did in the mid-1930s. FDR is the only President to have altered, fundamentally and irrevocably, the relationship between the citizen and the central government. That government assumed responsibility for the nation's economic health—the aggregate economic output—and for a minimum material well-being of the individual. If Reagan really wants to repeal those federal responsibilities (a repeal that would constitute a real revolution), he has never said so.

Clearly he did want to shrink government somewhat. And any shrinkage is an achievement that runs counter to the instinct of the animal. Professor James Q. Wilson of UCLA notes that the normal dynamic of politics is a process of addition: Candidates promise to add to government's repertory of benefits. Reagan has wanted to put a subtraction button on the great adding machine that the federal government has become. He thought the New Federalism might do that by devolving choices to lower governments. But that may not reduce the quantity of government in America (if "quantity" makes much sense in this regard, which I doubt). Conservatives say that governments closest to the people are the most accurate barometers of the real values of the people. What, then, do conservatives make of the fact that in recent years state and local governments have been growing faster than the federal government?

Conservatives say Americans should shape up and recur to the individualism that (conservatives say) made America great. Professor Samuel Beer, Harvard emeritus, argues that Reagan's individualism is both a theory of economic progress and a social ethic.[31] But whatever Reagan's private views are about what an ideal society might be, by 1987 this seemed clear: His budget-cutting is driven almost not at all by ideological animus against the form of government Democrats have largely built and Republicans such as Nixon and Ford have equably administered. Rather, the budget-cutting is driven by calculations—technical, not moral, judgments— necessary to restore economic growth while rearming. To the extent that rapid growth and rearmament are compatible with the post-FDR and post-LBJ government he inherited, it is to that extent that Reagan is a welfare state conservative.

How can a conservative be anything else? Conservative, as distinct from reactionary, politics values continuity and abhors radical ruptures with national patterns of action spanning fifty years.

Reagan the practitioner has been much more at ease with this than Reagan the rhetorician. Shortly after the Inauguration, Ronald Reagan met with congressional leaders on Capitol Hill, in private. He said some people were going to be surprised when they saw that federal spending would increase every year of his presidency. Reagan's aim in 1981 was almost the same as that of the most conservative quartet in the history of modern American government—Gerald Ford, Alan Greenspan, William Simon, Arthur Burns—who had been setting policy five years earlier. Their aim was to slow the rate of growth of the public sector relative to the private sector. Reagan's aim, put precisely, was to slow the rate of growth of the nondefense spending relative to defense spending, and the growth of government spending relative to the growth of the private sector.

Professor Beer pronounces Reagan a "New Deal conservative," a fact about Mr. Conservative that will have a long reverberation within the conservative party. Beer recalls a droll definition: "A conservative is a person who was a liberal when young and has not changed his mind." And Beer says that the key to understanding Reagan may be in understanding the essential difference between FDR's New Deal and LBJ's Great Society.

The New Deal was launched at about the time America

became a predominantly urban and industrial nation, and during an especially brutal business cycle. The New Deal aimed to alleviate deprivation—assumed to be temporary deprivation—produced by large but correctable events. The New Deal agenda was not complex: full employment and social insurance.

The Great Society was born in the midst of the boom. Its focus was intractable poverty amidst sustained economic growth. This was diagnosed to be deprivation with deep cultural roots, a diagnosis made with the thumping confidence characteristic of the social sciences in the 1960s. So the Great Society, more than the New Deal, aimed to do delicate, problematic things, like impart skills and alter motivations. This involved heavy emphasis on bureaucratic expertise (policy roles for social scientists) and public spending, especially federal aid to states and localities.

Social Security—an insurance rather than a services strategy of social amelioration—typified the New Deal. Federal aid (and accompanying regulations) typified the Great Society. The fact that Reagan's budget-cutting was directed first and hardest against federal aid to states and localities prompts Beer to describe Reagan as a New Deal conservative who is philosophically unsympathetic only to the Great Society outlay.

To get to the heart of Reagan's thinking, and perhaps to the key to the Republican future, the place to start is at the start. Return to noon, January 20, 1981.

Beer takes elegant exception to this assertion in President Reagan's 1981 inaugural address: "The federal government did not create the states; the states created the federal government." That proposition was central to the secessionists' argument before the Civil War. Lincoln argued that the Union created the states as states, and produced whatever independence and liberty they have. But what was at issue then was primarily a theory of authority. Today, the issue is a theory of purpose, a guide to the ends for which power should be used.

Reagan asserted the "compact theory" of the Union. Prior to the Civil War, that was used to justify "nullification" or state "interposition." According to that doctrine, the states, as authors of the federal government, are, individually, the proper judges of when it exceeds its authority. This argument was settled not by argument but by steel. But the essential political impulse of the compact theory lives today in the attitude of many conservatives toward the federal government.

America's challenge always has been to refute the theory that democracy is unsuited to a large society, because the central government, which should express national interests, will be dominated by parochial interests. That problem did not preoccupy Jefferson, because he envisioned a homogeneous, generally agricultural society, rather than the complicated commercial society Hamilton envisioned. But Hamilton lacked the poetry to express the romantic element essential to any potent concept of a nation. Lincoln had the poetry; so did Daniel Webster.

Defending the "national idea" in 1830, Daniel Webster cited the Delaware breakwater, an artificial harbor the federal government was constructing near the mouth of Delaware Bay. He argued that none of the neighboring states would have built it because it was not for the sole benefit of any one of them, so only the federal government could do it. But Webster—like Lincoln, and like another romantic nationalist, Edmund Burke—was unsatisfied merely with economic arguments for the central government's central role in American life. Webster urged a more organic concept of the nation, just as Burke had urged Britons to think of the nation as something more than a partnership agreement in trade, and just as Lincoln was to speak of "the mystic chords of memory, stretching from every battle-field, and patriot grave, to every living heart and hearthstone." [32]

The Civil War established federal supremacy as a fact, not a theory, and was followed by federal initiatives concerning banking, currency, land, transportation, tariffs, higher education, and other matters that prompted national integration. The next two great nationalizers were this century's two greatest Presidents.

Teddy Roosevelt called his program for countering the disintegrative effects of industrialism—inequalities and class conflict—the "New Nationalism." And, as Beer says, the thematic term of TR's cousin Franklin was the adjective "national." FDR nationalized economic policy: Henceforth the President would be held accountable for the economy's aggregate performance. He made a minimum material entitlement a national concern. And under him, regional politics increasingly yielded to the national politics of urban and class blocs.

Contemporary conservatism awaits its Burke or Webster—someone who, when he speaks of the nation's expression of itself through the national government, speaks with the soul of a poet rather than a corporate comptroller. Too many conservatives have a crabbed and dispiriting attitude toward the central government. Most Americans—their occasional rhetoric notwithstanding—do not. Watch families touring Washington; count the buses bringing high school students on class trips each spring. People visit New York; they make pilgrimages to Washington.

Conservatives worry too little about the disintegrative forces of the commercial dynamism they nurture. America has never suffered from too much unity or excessive national purposefulness. Conservative rhetoric aside, the federal interest has never been too strong.

Not surprisingly, the "natural" governing party—the Republicans after the Civil War, the Democrats after the crash of 1929—has been the party that has spoken with most conviction for using the federal government as an instrument of national integration.

Perhaps that criterion has changed, or should change, or is changing. Perhaps there is some other standard by which the voters shall decide which is the natural governing party. If so, the standard will be more felt than articulated. Then again, the role of natural governing party may be up for grabs in 1988. If so, it is the Democratic party's last chance to get its act together and take it on the road. So it is time to turn our attention to the Democrats.

# DEMOCRATS

When Earl Weaver was manager of the Baltimore Orioles he would charge at umpires shouting, "Are you gonna get any better, or is *this* it?" Many Democrats, weary of watching the Democratic party flounder in presidential competition, are ready to rise up and shout like that. During the last forty years the party's fall has been long and hard. Has the party hit bottom so hard it will rise on the bounce? Time—actually, 1988—will tell. But one thing already is known. Pride goeth before the fall, and before its fall the Democratic party was full of pride.

Dean Acheson, perhaps the most formidable Democrat when the party was most formidable, was once asked by a friend, "You are intelligent and experienced. And yet you are a Democrat. How can this be?" The question stirred in Acheson ruminations that he turned into a book thirty years ago, *A Democrat Looks at His Party.*[1] Acheson, ever insouciant, said, essentially, that he was a Democrat because, obviously, almost all intelligent people were. Acheson, who could be

94

charming even while being condescending, was inclined to believe, as others have, that not all conservatives are stupid but that all stupid people are conservative.

The Democratic party during the Eisenhower years often was condescending but did not carry it off with Acheson's éclat. It was the condescension of a party that was breaking its lance, and its liberal heart, with Adlai Stevenson. He expressed the essence of Democratic condescension in his remark that when Eisenhower came to office the New Dealers were replaced by the car dealers. The remark was witty but also complacent and self-congratulatory, a symptom of liberalism becoming overripe. Eisenhower did come to office and held it for eight years. Democrats had the leisure to hone their condescension because they were not busy running the country.

Democratic presidential candidates have won a majority of the popular vote only twice in the last ten elections (Johnson and Carter.) Beginning with 1952, the Republican dominance of Democrats in electoral votes is 3,245 to 1,518. Since Eisenhower entered politics, Democrats have lost six of nine elections, have received 12 percent fewer popular votes (Democrat 305,030,826 to GOP 347,268,238) than the Republicans. Just under one-quarter of today's electorate was eligible to vote in 1952. That means three-quarters have voted only in what is, at the presidential level, a Republican era.

Horace Busby, a wise political consultant whose pocket calculator never sleeps, reports that in 1980 some voter cast the billionth vote cast since 1856 for a presidential candidate of the Republican or Democratic parties (more than half a billion have been cast since 1952). In this, "the oldest continuous political competition in the world," the popular vote split has been amazingly even. As of 1984, each party has received more than 500 million votes—Republicans 51 percent, Democrats 49 percent.

Starting in 1860 Republicans lead in elections won, twenty to twelve. And 54 percent of the electoral votes have gone to

Republicans, 46 percent to Democrats. There have been eras of lopsided dominance. From 1860 to 1928 Republicans won 61 percent of the electoral votes. From 1932 through 1948 Democrats had the strongest dominance yet recorded: 83 percent. In the five elections beginning in 1968 Republicans have won 78 percent of the electoral votes. The 1932–1948 Democratic dominance was really FDR's one-man show. In 1948 Truman did not even get a majority of the popular vote. (Since 1944 no northern liberal Democratic candidate for President has received a majority of the popular vote. The only two Democrats who have—LBJ in 1964 and Carter, barely, in 1976—were from states of the Confederacy.) If a Republican wins in 1988, Republicans will govern at least until 1992, by which time they will have governed twenty-eight out of forty years.

Busby has propounded a theory of the Republicans' electoral college "lock." The facts of it are as follows.

The post-war political era can reasonably be said to have begun in 1952, when Truman, a creature of FDR's will (or, more accurately, FDR's whim) retired. In the nine elections beginning in 1952, thirty-nine states have voted Republican five times or more. Those thirty-nine have a total of 441 electoral votes, 171 more than the 270 needed to win. Thirty-three states, with 322 electoral votes, have gone Republican in six of those nine elections. Seventeen states with 143 electoral votes have gone Republican in eight of the nine.[2] Monomaniacal Arizona has voted Republican in all nine.

The Democratic party has no comparable base of states strongly disposed toward it. Only the District of Columbia (3) and two states, Minnesota (10) and West Virginia (6), with a total of just 19 electoral votes, have voted Democratic in six of the nine elections. Seven states (Arkansas, 6; Georgia, 12; Hawaii, 4; Maryland, 10; Massachusetts, 13; North Carolina, 13; and Rhode Island, 4) have voted Democratic in *only* five of the nine. But those states have a total of just 62 electoral votes. Therefore, against the 39 "five-or-*more*-of nine" Republican states with their 441 electoral votes, the Democrats' "five-or-*more*-of-nine" states and the District of Columbia have a paltry 81 electoral votes.

Who is the most potent Democrat of the last two decades? Jimmy Carter. Do not scoff. You can look it up. In a span of five elections (1968, 1972, 1976, 1980, 1984) he is the only Democrat to win more than 43 percent of the vote.

Three times since 1952 Republicans have elected Presidents. Each time they have re-elected them by increased margins. Democrats have not done that since FDR. Before FDR, Democrats last did it with Andrew Jackson and Martin Van Buren in the 1832 and 1836 elections. However, Democrats looking at 1988 derive hope from what Nelson Polsby calls the "landslide sequence."[3] In the last fourteen elections ten were in such sequences. That is, five (1936, 1956, 1964, 1972, 1984) were thumping re-elections for Presidents to second terms (LBJ in 1964 standing in for JFK). The follow-on to 1984 is, of course, unknown. But in three of the other four cases (1956, 1964, 1972) in the election following the landslide the party that had won the landslide lost the presidency.

Everett Carll Ladd, senior editor of *Public Opinion*, notes there are twenty-three N(2)FR(2) states. Such states went for Nixon twice, Ford once, Reagan twice. Those states have 202 electoral votes. How many HMC(2)M states (those that went for Humphrey, McGovern, Carter twice, Mondale) are there? Zero. Only the District of Columbia (3 votes) has been faithful. Let us assume that those 205 electoral votes (202 + 3) can be considered locked up by the two parties. That leaves 333 up for grabs. Republicans need to grab only one of the five to win, Democrats need to grab four of five. Only once in four decades—against Goldwater—has the Democrat won a majority of white middle-class voters. Mondale lost two-thirds of them. Down South, he lost three-quarters. Except in 1964, independents have favored the Republican since 1952.[4]

In his 1980 concession statement, Vice President Walter Mondale said: "The people have peacefully wielded their staggering power." No one has been as blasted as Mondale by that power. Adlai Stevenson lost twice by a cumulative electoral vote total of 899 to 162. In Mondale's last two times on a national ticket he has lost 1,014 to 62. The Mondale-Ferraro ticket was the most ideologically uniform and markedly liberal ticket in memory, yet only 21 percent of the participants in the 1984 Democratic primaries identified themselves as liberals. One-fourth called themselves independents and in the primaries Mondale got only one-fourth of that one-fourth.

Mondale, the choice of just 39 percent of the voters in Democratic primaries, had the task of preventing the fourth Republican victory in five elections. Only three times in this century has an incumbent President been defeated, and each defeat involved extraordinary circumstances. In 1912 Republicans split and Taft finished third behind Wilson and Teddy Roosevelt's "Bull Moose" candidacy. In 1932 the Depression destroyed Hoover. In 1980 . . . well, optimism is the indispensible ingredient in American politics, and it has been said that Carter's was America's first pessimistic administration.

California is a symbol of American optimism. It is therefore indicative that voters rejected Mondale emphatically in California's primary. Democrats have lost the state in eight of the last nine elections, and California has been the biggest winner of Reagan's presidency. Between 1982 and 1986, defense spending generated approximately 700,000 jobs there. California received more than 20 percent of all defense primary contracts over $25,000, an average of $26 billion per year, almost twice the amount received in 1980.

(Historian Stephen E. Ambrose, author of biographies of Eisenhower and Nixon, also is the author of what he calls the California Principle in Presidential Politics. It is that Democrats win a majority of the votes only when the Republicans do not put a Californian on the ticket. In the last nine elections the Democrats have tied one (1960) and won two (1964 and 1976). There has been a Californian on all six of the victorious Republican tickets, Nixon in 1952, 1956, 1968, and 1972, and Reagan in 1980 and 1984. There also was a Californian (Nixon) on the Republican ticket in the 1960 tie. California has gone Republican in all six Republican victories. Ten elections ago, in 1948, the Republicans lost the White House even though they had a Californian—Earl Warren—on the ticket. But California was then just becoming a mega-state. Ambrose believes that the Republican nominee in 1988 would be wise to pick a Californian as running mate.)

As the Republican party has grown, it has acquired problems associated with incompatible, or at least mutually incomprehensible, constituencies, such as Yuppies and evangelicals. But more important than the Republican problems associated with Republican growth is the Democratic problem that becomes worse because of Republican growth. As the Republican party grows, the Democratic party becomes more liberal. This reflects the political chemistry of concentration. As moderately conservative Democrats drift away to the Republican party, or just to disassociation from the Democratic party, the ratio of liberals to all others in the Democratic party rises. This makes it steadily more difficult for a moderately conservative Democrat to win a presidential nomination. And that hastens the flight of the less liberal Democrats. And so it goes.

Or does it? The problem is not simply too much liberalism. William Schneider, of the American Enterprise Institute, notes that recent Democratic nomination contests have not been left-versus-right contests, or young-versus-old contests, rather they have been "insiders" versus "outsiders."[5]

The modern history (and the decline) of the Democratic party began in 1968, in Chicago. There, Hubert Humphrey (assisted by a protégé named Walter Mondale) defeated forces outside the party establishment, many of them actually outside the convention hall, in the streets. In 1972 and 1976, the nominations went to outsiders. The 1972 nominee was George McGovern, the candidate of disaffected Democrats who vowed in 1968 to take control of the Democratic party away from the "establishment." McGovern, the Senator-as-outsider, defeated Ed Muskie and others who competed for endorsements from members of that establishment. In 1976 Carter defeated Henry Jackson and others while boasting that he was untainted by Washington connections, habits, or assumptions. In 1984 Mondale, the insiders' revenge, defeated Gary Hart, one of whose new ideas was that insiders are burnt-out cases incapable of entertaining, let alone originating, new ideas.

Mondale certainly was the insider's insider. When John Glenn, an intelligent and personable man, failed in his bid for the 1984 Democratic nomination, a supporter said, "John's problem is that he's a 90 percenter."[6] The supporter meant that Glenn would go out of his way, but not all the way, to please the party's constituencies. Mondale would. His problem was that most Americans do not think of themselves as members of the Democratic party's component constituencies and they perceived him, to his disadvantage, as a "100 percenter."

By the summer of 1984, one discouraged Democrat said Mondale's strategy had become his message. Another said Mondale's method mirrored his mind, in this sense: Mondale did not think in terms of individuals. Rather, he thought that everyone is a member of a group, and every group has its organization, and every organization has a leader with whom you make arrangements.

To be elected President in the 1980s you must get 55 million Americans to vote for you. Now, consider: What do 55 million Americans agree about? Precious little. Or, to be more precise, precious little other than propositions couched in a high level of generality. Mondale tried to cobble together the 55 million from lots of groups. Against Mondale, as against Carter, Reagan took a different approach. Reaganism is politics-as-evangelism, calling forth a majority with a hymn to general values. Mondaleism is politics-as-masonry, building a majority brick by brick.

A pervasive uneasiness with Mondale's approach to politics gave rise to the extraordinary fling that Democratic primary voters had with Gary Hart in the late winter and early spring of 1984. For six weeks or so he was a full-fledged fad. Within ten days after Hart's upset of Mondale in New Hampshire, the nation was treated to the And-He-Was-A-Teenage-Existentialist! stage in the apotheosis of the candidate. One of Hart's professors at Bethany Nazarene College in Bethany, Oklahoma, said Kierkegaard had an "explosive" effect on young Gary's intellect. Fear and trembling in Oklahoma, 1955. But my hero, and the winner of the No-Damned-Nonsense-About-Merit trophy, is the man who, asked why he was supporting Hart, said Hart was the only one he had not heard of a month ago.

Hart had not been silent since reaching the Senate in 1975, but people outside Colorado were not paying attention. So, when he suddenly got the nation's attention in March, 1984, he was known primarily as that thin young fellow who was not Mondale. It was not Hart's fault, but in that moment of sudden attention he was like that little tub of vaguely milk-like gunk that comes with airline coffee. It is labeled a non-dairy product. Fine: We know what it is *non*, but what is it? It was not until May, 1987, that Americans decided, with the help of Donna Rice, that they knew enough and did not like what they knew. But for a while in the spring of 1984 Hart was America's Rorschach test: Folks saw in him what their psyches craved. Listening to voters describe him contradictorily, I thought of Hamlet having fun with Polonius:

*Hamlet:* Do you see yonder cloud that's almost in shape of a camel?
*Polonius:* . . . 'tis like a camel indeed.
*Hamlet:* Methinks it is like a weasel.

*Polonius:* It is backed like a weasel.
*Hamlet:* Or like a whale.
*Polonius:* Very like a whale.[7]

Mondale was very like a utility infielder, relying more on versatility than any spectacular virtuosity. He was a man for his party's big battalions, such as organized labor, and clients of the public sector, such as the public-education lobby (the National Education Association). By 1980, after a decade of reforms to "democratize" the party, the Democratic convention represented the government as an interest group. That convention was dominated by persons who provide or receive public services. The largest bloc of delegates—311 (and 170 alternates)—were NEA members. Mondale, with his penchant for the politics of the organized interests, was a natural nominee of such a convention.

However, in 1984 some Democratic strategists had a theory about winning with the help of the least organized Americans. The theory was that unregistered people comprise a huge reservoir of potential Democratic votes. The assumption was that these people are not registered because they were disaffected. So if they are once registered, they will storm to the polls and there register their seething resentments against the incumbent President. The theory got a fair test. In 1984, thanks to efforts by both parties, an astonishing 12 million more people were registered to vote than in 1980. But only four million more bothered to vote. And evidently 11 million people have guilty consciences about not voting: Ninety-three million people voted in 1984, but polls show that 104 million say they voted. So much for the notion that 80 percent of those who register also vote. As David Osborne notes, the 80 percent figure remains true for people who bother to register themselves but not for people who are snagged by volunteers in supermarket parking lots. Osborne's axiom is: "New voters do not create new politics; new politics create new voters."[8] Not surprisingly, new voters vote in different ways at different times. In 1964 new voters went 88 percent for Johnson. In 1980 new voters split evenly between Carter and Reagan. In 1984 they did about what the country did: 60 to 40 for Reagan. So to the extent that Democrats helped run up registration figures in the hope of harnessing disaffection, they were severely disappointed.

It is true that in 1984, in the teeth of the Reagan gale, Democrats won 65 percent of all contested elections. It is true, but it is cold comfort for clear-sighted Democrats. They know that "trickle-down politics" works, and is working against them. Repeated Republican successes in presidential contests cannot be hermetically sealed at that level. A party that wins the White House consistently enough will, in time, win the courthouse. Ours is a presidential system. The presidency is the agenda-setting and tone-setting institution from which radiate influences that permeate all levels of politics.

Perhaps the durable Democratic strength below the presidential level is primarily a result of incumbency. If incumbents had been barred from the ballot in 1984, Republicans probably would have captured even the House of Representatives. However, the rounded picture of the 1984 voting at all levels of government demonstrates that a majority of Americans are comfortable voting for Democrats, if the party refrains from chasing them away. It is arguable that the presidency is different. Perhaps for lesser offices voters look for a kind of diligence associated with Democrats, who like government in all its concreteness. Perhaps voters think Republicans are better at articulating (in Eisenhower's case it was more a matter of exemplifying than articulating) general values that amount to presidential vision.

Many Democrats say that the Republican run of successes is a fluke produced by a series of weak Democratic nominees. But in the last four elections the Democratic party has tried to sell the country McGovern, Carter twice (successfully only against an accidental President), and Mondale. Four such "aberrations" consecutively are not aberrations. They reflect a single strong propensity to misread the electorate's mood.

However, the moving finger of the American electorate writes messages that are always changing and often are difficult to decipher. That certainly was the case in 1986.

When the cloister-like calm of American life had been momentarily restored by the end of the 1986 election season, a large, echoing fact could be quietly contemplated: In 1976 there was a majority party; by 1986 there was not. There was rough parity between the parties as the 1988 campaign for supremacy commenced.

In two fields of 1986 competition, the party with the most to lose (the Republican party defending more Senate seats and the Democratic party defending more governorships) lost more. Republicans could take some comfort from this, for several reasons.

First, to be blunt, fewer of the inadequacies of the Republican Senate "coattail class" of 1980 proved fatal than could have. Second, the "sixth-year itch" made retention of Senate control by Republicans unlikely. In the last six elections in a President's sixth year (1918, 1926, 1938, 1958, 1966, 1974), the party not holding the White House has won between four (Republicans, 1966) and thirteen (Democrats, 1958) Senate seats. The average gain has been seven. So in 1986 Republicans were going to lose the Senate even if they did as well as any party has done in the six "sixth-year" elections: four losses. In fact the Republicans lost eight, one more than the average.

In 1982, a change of just 31,090 votes—a submicroscopic total—spread over five states (Delaware, Vermont, Rhode Island, Nevada, Wyoming) would have restored Democrats to Senate control. Furthermore, Democrats would already have controlled the Senate then if in 1980 just 34,000 votes spread over five states (Idaho, Arizona, North Carolina, New Hampshire, Georgia) had gone the other way. In 1980, Republicans gained twelve seats although Democratic Senate candidates got nearly 3 million more votes, largely because of landslides for John Glenn in Ohio and Alan Cranston in California.

Regarding House races, one reason presidential landslides exert such slight pull is that Americans have become adept at ticket-splitting. In 1984, Reagan carried 372 of the 435 congressional districts, but Republicans won only 181. By contrast, in Warren Harding's 1920 landslide, there were only approximately eleven such splits. But the electorate always has been given to a split vision of political responsibilities. The evidence of this is a two-tier political tradition.

Busby notes that since 1860, Republicans have won twenty of thirty-two presidential elections, and by the end of 1988 will have held the White House 65 percent of the time. So we have, Busby says, two "60-40" political systems: One in Congress, one involving the presidency. This may be largely because Congress is considered to be essentially a services-dispensing institution, and Democrats dispense with more zest and attentiveness than Republicans. However, Busby has an additional (although perhaps related) explanation of the "two-tier" phenomenon. For many years, he says, the nation's forty most populous counties have had at least 100 members of the House—slightly more today—and Republicans have not had more than 5 of the 100. Busby believes the Democrats' domination of the House is based less on liberalism than on ethnicity. There are, he says, just too few Republican ethnic candidates.[9]

Of course some people might argue that Busby has got things backward, that Republicans have too few ethnic constituencies. Such people would say that Reagan's great achievement for the Republican party was to carry many such constituencies twice, and one of the fascinating questions about 1988 is whether there is a Republican candidate who can consolidate Republican gains in such constituencies.

Whatever the answer to that question turns out to be, it certainly is the case that ticket-splitting in a Republican presidential era works to the advantage of Democrats all the way down the ballot. In the minor leagues of American politics Democrats have been more than holding their own. In the 1986 competition for approximately 7,500 state legislative seats, Democrats, who were already well ahead, gained 180 seats and now control sixty-eight of the ninety-eight partisan legislative chambers, a gain of five chambers. (Peculiar Nebraska, with its unicameral and nonpartisan legislature, does not count, except to Nebraskans.) In politics as in baseball what happens in the minor leagues matters because that is where the big leaguers grow. Attractive state legislators often get promoted to the national legislature.

However, ours is, to repeat, a presidential system in the sense that Presidents set the national agenda and the tone of public life. In a Republican presidential era, this gives some help to Republicans in the lower reaches of politics. This Republican "trickling down" of presidential effects competes with the Democratic "bubbling up" of proven electoral talent.

Another lesson of the 1986 elections is that the electorate knows how to avoid being manipulated. In 1986, Republicans invested extravagant hopes in their advantage at fund-raising and their ability to finance the blocking and tackling of politics—the computerized mailing and phoning that identifies, contacts, and goads particular voters to the polls. However, one heartening lesson of the 1986 results is that television, technology, and Niagaras of cash reach a point of sharply declining utility. Democrats were outspent, Republicans were out-voted.

In retrospect one of the most interesting Senate races, was, in the contesting of it, among the dullest. It was in New York, where Alfonse D'Amato, the Republican incumbent, easily won a second term by trouncing Mark Green, 57.9 percent to 41.9 percent.

Green charged that D'Amato is "a person of no consequence in the city of results [Washington]." But Green thought of consequence in terms of national reputation on progressive issues, as exemplified by such New York Senators as Wagner, Javits, Robert Kennedy, and Moynihan. Green said D'Amato is only interested in constituent service and showering New York with pork. To many ears, that charge did not sound wounding.

Green's optimism about his election was grounded in this fact: New York had never elected a conservative Senator in a two-way race. James Buckley won in 1970 running on the Conservative party ticket against liberals on the Democratic and Republican tickets. D'Amato won in 1980 by beating the incumbent Republican, Jacob Javits, in the primary, then beating a liberal Democrat by 1 percent, getting just 45 percent. He won by 80,000 votes while Javits took 664,544 on the Liberal party ticket. In a two-person race, D'Amato would have lost.

But Reagan has carried New York twice. How liberal is it? Michael Barone says New York no longer has a left-wing vote larger than that of all other states. He says New York is perhaps 3 to 5 percentage points more Democratic than the national average. New York pioneered the welfare state and pushed it to—beyond, actually—the fiscal limits. The worst excesses were committed by Republicans, Nelson Rockefeller and John Lindsay. Today, Barone writes, New York's basic constituencies have a Democratic heritage but are displeased "with the cultural liberalism that is so attractive to so many Manhattan voters"[10] and interested in disciplining and preserving, but not expanding, the welfare state that was established for their forebears.

Green thought his nomination revealed the resiliency of liberalism. However, it may actually have illustrated a syndrome of a party in trouble. In 1982, more than 1 million people voted in the Democrats' Senate primary. In 1986, fewer than 500,000 did. As the Democratic party's liberalism causes many centrists to drift away, the residue that dominates primaries becomes more intensely liberal. So the drifting accelerates.

But—it cannot be said too often—politics is not like particle physics. It is not done in an accelerator; it is not governed by physical laws or a cadre of political physicists. And neither is it a branch of psychology.

This age, which is full of faith in psychology, thinks that anything a person does, from the way he dreams to the way he eats artichokes, reveals, to the tutored eye, his moods. So, given the science of polling, many people probably think it is a snap to decode the nation's mood and forecast its immediate political future.

But it is not. So we try to achieve predictive powers by discerning patterns in the past that may extend into the future. In his new book, *The Cycles of American History,* Arthur M. Schlesinger, Jr., distinguished historian and unreconstructed Democrat, argues that America has alternating rhythms, periods of activist government followed by periods of preoccupation with private interests.[11]

The minimalist government of the late nineteenth-century Gilded Age was followed by the activism of the turn-of-the-century Progressive Era. That yielded to the conservatism of the 1920s, which was followed by Roosevelt-Truman activism. Then came the conservatism of Ike's 1950s, then Kennedy's call to get "moving again" and LBJ's Great Society. In 1968 there began another twenty-year cycle of conservatism, Nixon through Reagan. And now?

Schlesinger says Theodore Roosevelt and Woodrow Wilson infected a generation of young people like Franklin and Eleanor Roosevelt and Harry Truman who, in maturity, produced their own activism. FDR in turn had political offspring such as JFK and LBJ. Schlesinger says: "In the same way the age of Kennedy touched and inspired a new generation. That generation's time is yet to come."[12] If Schlesinger is correct about such cycles, the time for the political children of Kennedy arrives in 1988.

Reviewing Schlesinger's book in *The New Republic*, Professor Alan Brinkley of Harvard notes that even if political disjunctions can be discerned at, say, twenty-year intervals, that fact does not necessarily yield a theory with predictive powers. Three large events that drove American politics in new directions—two world wars and the Depression—occurred when they did for reasons unrelated to the existence of any American cycle. Patterns detected in the past may be mere coincidences like, Brinkley notes, "the causally meaningless fact that Presidents elected at 20-year intervals since 1840 have all, until now, died in office."[13]

Schlesinger's cycle theory has predictive value only if there is, in Brinkley's words, an internal dynamic that makes the cycle self-generating. Schlesinger says there is. It is the ability of activist leaders to seed the future with inspired young people. Schlesinger says: ". . . it is the generational experience that serves as the mainspring of the political cycle."[14]

Schlesinger's theory of approximately twenty-year cycles points to a consummation he devoutly desires—a liberal restoration in 1988. But historical rhythms are in the eye of the beholder and John Sears, veteran of Nixon and Reagan campaigns, has a theory of national character from which he derives his own theory of the oscillations of America's politics.

Americans, he says, are naturally optimistic and assume that change means improvement. Such optimism translates into support for whichever party promises an era of change. But the nation has not always assumed that change results only from activist government.

In 1861, the infant GOP took charge of preserving the Union and, in the process, ended slavery. The nation then entered an era of hyperactivity—immigration, industrialization, closing the frontier, building railroads. The nation identified the GOP as the party with an ideology (minimal

government, *laissez-faire*) conducive to rapid change. The
GOP dominated politics for seventy-two years. Between 1860
and 1932 there were just two Democratic Presidents, Grover
Cleveland and Woodrow Wilson, and both were results of
Republican schisms.

In 1932 the Democratic party acquired, first by default and
soon through action, the status of the party of change. This
was the result of the second great crisis since the Civil War—
the Depression. There were two Republican episodes between 1932 and 1980. The Eisenhower ascendancy was a
national pause for breath. It was not the result of a reassess-
ment by the electorate of the matter of which party stood for
change. Nixon's two victories were very early signs of the
gathering difficulties within the Democratic party. The 1980
election punctuated a crisis of confidence that began with
Vietnam and Watergate and culminated in the sense of impo-
tence produced by high inflation and the Iranian hostage crisis. The 1980 mandate was for less government energy
domestically and more internationally.

Notice the difference between John Sears's and Schlesinger's perceived rhythms. Sears, a veteran of many Republican campaigns, directed Reagan's campaign in 1976 and in
1980 through the New Hampshire primary. He stresses the
nation's penchant for social change, which sometimes has
been, but at other times has not been, identified with an activist federal government. The generally conservative policies
of the last three decades of the nineteenth century coincided
with the most transforming changes (industrialism, immigration) in American history.

If, as Sears says, the American constant is a craving for
change, the question for Schlesinger is whether in 1988, unlike the case in 1980, government will be considered an ini-
tiator of change rather than an inhibitor of America's creative
energies. In American politics the desire for change is problematic for the Democratic party. Liberalism has done least
well in the regions undergoing the most rapid change, the

regions with the most crackling energy. The Democratic party has had trouble with its courtship of two regions, the South and the West. It has not been able to make that courtship compatible with the task of holding its base in the Northeast.

A presidential candidate has two crucial resources—time and money. If nothing is tied down, time and money cannot be economized. The Democrats' problem in 1980 and 1984 was that nothing was tied down—no region, not even the Northeast. When the liberal party cannot assume a base of support in the most liberal region, or the conservative party in the most conservative region, everything begins to unravel. To hold the candidate's natural base, he must go there and say, loud and clear, the things the dominant constituencies want to hear. And that gets him in trouble in the places where he can least stand trouble.

This, by the way, is the basis of the case for Democrats' doing something that seems, at first blush, peculiar—nominating a northeastern liberal. The point, says John Sears, "is to get into the race with some votes"—some electoral votes. If you can come out of the starting blocks with, say, New York, Massachusetts, Rhode Island, perhaps Pennsylvania and New Jersey in hand or leaning strongly your way, at least you have something to take for granted, something to build on.[15]

But there is no need for Democrats to plan on holding on to the Northeast unless they find a way to compete in the South.

In various eras various regions have been considered the key to political dominance. Most recently the South has been considered the most crucial region. After the 1986 elections Republicans held five governorships in the eleven states of the Confederacy. That fact denotes this fact: Today, for the first time since the two-party competition began in the second half of the nineteenth century, both parties are competitive in every region.

It is northern parochialism and condescension to say that

the South is "joining" the mainstream. The South is a—perhaps is the—mainstream, in size and disposition. The current House of Representatives is the first in which a majority of seats are not from the states that won the Civil War. Republican successes in the rising regions—the South and the West —have tempted, or forced, Democrats to concentrate on the Northeast and industrial Midwest. This regionalism partially explains today's unusually divergent views of the two parties concerning the country's condition and the government's agenda. After the 1990 census, the eleven southern states from Virginia to Texas probably will have 128 seats in the House of Representatives (128 seats is almost 30 percent of the 435 House seats) and 148 electoral votes (55 percent of the 270 electoral votes needed to win the White House).

The South is the nation's least urban region (38 percent of southerners live in rural areas, compared with 22 percent of other Americans), the poorest region (although no longer by much: personal income is 86 percent of that of the rest of the nation) and it has the highest percentage of blacks (20 percent, compared with 12 percent nationally). Today the sleepy South is wide awake. It is the most dynamic region, and dynamism means homogenization and the dilution of regional differences. There is irony in this process. In Georgia 70 percent of recent growth has been within 100 miles of the Atlanta airport or within 25 miles of an interstate highway. This is where Republicans are winning. They are beneficiaries of economic dynamism generated by two huge public works. The irony of that is, no doubt, lost on them.

As William C. Harard, a political scientist, said of the modern South, the cotton moved west, the farmer moved to town, the townsfolk moved to the suburbs, blacks moved north, and Yankees went south. In 1988 everybody is going south for the two weeks after the New Hampshire primary. I am using the word "everybody" the way it was used by a famous movie critic after the 1972 election. She exclaimed in bewilderment, "But everybody I know voted for McGovern!" By "every-

body" going south I mean our gang—the journalists and political hangers-on—drawn like iron filings by the magnet of
the southern primary.

The southern regional primary, coming hard on the heels
of New Hampshire's primary, will select a number of
delegates equal to nearly 60 percent of the total needed to
nominate. The architects of this mega-event are Democratic-
controlled southern state legislatures. What have they
wrought? Neither they nor anyone else knows. Among the
many things that are unclear about it is this elemental matter:
No one knows who will vote where. Eight of the participating
states have open primaries, so voters will be free to choose
which party's primary to play in. It is easy to imagine a cir-
cumstance in which this would defeat one purpose of the
regional primary. The principle purpose of the southern
Democrats who proposed this regional primary was to increase the influence of their region in the party's nominating
process. But suppose the "slingshot effect" of Iowa and New
Hampshire slings two liberals toward the South. Suppose the
regional primary becomes, on the Democratic side, essentially a referendum on the candidates who finished first and
second in New Hampshire. Suppose those two are, say,
Dukakis and Simon. Conservative Democrats might wrinkle
their noses and curl their lips and migrate to the Republican
side of the primary, leaving the Democratic primary largely
in the possession of liberals. The black vote would remain
loyal to the Democratic party and would become even more
powerful in that primary. All white candidates other than the
first and second place finishers in New Hampshire might be
too short of cash to continue, but Jesse Jackson's campaign, if
it is like his magical mystery tour of 1984, will be running on
adrenalin, churches and free media. It is conceivable that
Jackson could win the regional primary that southern Democrats hoped would move the party toward moderation.

However, whatever the outcome, the existence of the primary proves that the South has risen, yet again. Or, to be

exact, it means that the rise of the South has at last been recognized by a slow learner, the Democratic party.

In 1948 the Democratic party won with Harry Truman, a man from a state that had considerable Confederate sympathies—the state in which Dred Scott went to court. Since 1948 the Democrats have won just three presidential elections, with three different candidates, and two (Johnson and Carter) were from states of the Confederacy. The Democratic party, says William Schneider, has become less populist and more liberal as the country has tended toward what Reagan embodies and the South admires—a mixture of populism and conservatism.[16] Populism involves expansive faith in the masses, sentimental celebration of the common man, suspicion of meritocracies and other hierarchies, including resentment of a regulating central government of the sort associated with northern liberalism.

If the Democratic party is going to come back to presidential power, it must come to terms with the South's conservatism. Since Franklin Roosevelt's death, no non-southern Democratic presidential candidate has won 50 percent of the national vote. In fact, FDR is the only northern liberal Democrat ever to win a popular vote majority. While Mondale, the most recent northern liberal sent South, was carrying just seven southern congressional districts, relatively conservative Democrats were winning seventy-three southern seats. The "solid South" was solidly for FDR, but he would have won all four of his elections without a single southern vote. In three of the last five elections (1968, 1972, 1984) the Democrats did not put a southerner on the ticket. In those elections the Democrats carried one southern state—Texas— once. The Democrats' three-election score in the eleven states of the old Confederacy was: 1 win, 32 losses.

Three times the Democratic party has nominated a liberal northern Protestant for President and a liberal northern Catholic for Vice President. Each time the electorate has given that choice a negative review. In 1968 the Humphrey-

Muskie ticket got 43 percent of the vote. In 1972 McGovern-Shriver got 38 percent. In 1984 Mondale-Ferraro got 41 percent.[17] Since 1964—since the nomination and election of the first southerner since the Civil War—only one Democratic candidate has won a majority of southern votes. He was Carter of Georgia, and not even he won a majority of white southerners.

No Republican has won the presidency without carrying Ohio. No Democrat has won without carrying Texas. However, Virginia is especially symptomatic of Democratic problems. Since 1948, only one Democratic presidential candidate (Lyndon Johnson, in 1964) has carried Virginia. Furthermore, as David Broder notes,

> In every presidential election since 1956, the candidate who has won the largest number of electoral votes in the 11 southern states has walked into the White House. That is true of no other region. The Midwest and the West voted for losers in 1960 and 1976; the Northeast in 1968.[18]

So in 1988 it will have been nine elections—thirty-six years—since the South backed the losing horse. But before Republicans sigh with happiness they should be reminded that the southern heart is fickle. Between 1964 and 1984 only Virginia among southern states voted for the same party (the GOP) three consecutive times. Neither the Republicans nor the Democrats have won the South three times in a row. In 1988 the Republicans will be trying for their third consecutive victory.

Of course the South is not the Democrats' only region of difficulty. West of the Mississippi, the Democrats carried none of the twenty-four states in 1972; they carried six in 1976, two in 1980, none in 1984—a four-election record of eight won, eighty-eight lost. Shortly after the 1980 election, Mondale told this writer that he and Carter saw a negative omen in the fact that immediately after the Republican convention Reagan moved his campaign headquarters from near Los Angeles airport to Arlington, Virginia, a short drive from Washington's National Airport. The move suggested to Mondale and Carter that Reagan assumed he could essentially take for granted the support of the electorate from about two-thirds of the land area of the country.

Between 1940 and 1980 the Northeast and Midwest have lost 58 House seats. Of those lost, 6 went to the South. Of the 52 that went to the West, 34 went to California. As the 1990 census approaches, the South and West lead the Northeast and Midwest, 227 to 208. From 1980 through 1986 the nation's population grew by 14.5 million, and 90 percent of that total—13.2 million—has been added to the South and West. Those regions should gain 19 seats in the next census, to lead 246 to 189. When Democrats grow weary of worrying about the South, they can worry about the West. But, then, if they solve their problem with the South, they will have gone a long way toward solving their problem with the West. This is because the South's susceptibility to Republican wooing is grounded in resentments the West shares. One is the belief that the federal government has become an inhibitor of economic dynamism, sacrificing economic growth for such goals as environmental protection or distributive justice programs. Another longstanding resentment derives from the durable belief that under any administration the "permanent government"—the federal bureaucracy—is dominated by eastern liberals who too much enjoy bossing around other regions, telling them how to run their schools (the South) and what to do with their land and water (the West).

The Democrats' difficulties with the South and West reflect regional rejections of certain ideological tendencies. Regionalism is a familiar phenomenon in the politics of this continental nation. But it is a phenomenon decreasing in importance as the nation becomes more homogenized by the mobility of its population and shared journalistic and entertainment experiences. Increasingly, the crucial variables in contemporary politics are not geographic but demographic. Today's axiom is: As the baby boom generation goes, so goes the nation.

Generational thinking is once again in vogue, as it was in 1960 when John Kennedy talked about passing a torch to a new generation possessing "vigor" (the implication being that the presiding generation—Eisenhower's—lacked vigor). Eisenhower and his generation defeated the Axis and launched the recovery of the world—not bad for people supposedly deficient in vigor. However, Kennedy also had the good fortune to be running against Nixon, who was only three years older than Kennedy but seemed to have been born middle-aged and carrying a briefcase. It is arguable, from the perspective of the 1980s, that Eisenhower and Kennedy were more united by shared experiences—the World War and the beginning of the Cold War—than they were divided by the age difference that Kennedy stressed in his generational appeal.

Still, Kennedy does hold the age-reversal record for Presidents. He was twenty-seven years younger than the man he replaced.[19] That record could be broken in 1988 by the election of, for example, Bruce Babbitt or Sam Nunn, both born in 1938, or Joseph Biden (1942), or Albert Gore (1948). Most of the men mentioned as Democratic candidates for the 1988 nomination were not eligible to vote when Eisenhower ran for his second term. (Granted, that was the Dark Age, before eighteen-year-olds could vote.) Sixty percent of today's electorate became eligible to vote after John Kennedy was elected, and more than 10 percent were not born when he was assassinated.[20]

The baby boom cohort has a strong sense of generational cohesion grounded in a popular culture produced in response to the sheer mass—and purchasing power—of the baby boom market. Movies like *The Return of the Secaucus Seven, The Big Chill,* and *American Graffiti* cater to the powerful sense of identity among the 76 million baby boom Americans born between 1946 and 1964. In 1988 they could constitute 60 percent of the electorate. A candidate who wins, say, a 57 to 43 split of that group probably becomes President.

A pioneer of boomerology—the study of them—is Pat Caddell, Democratic consultant. He says this generation is uniquely "self-contained." Because of its "critical-mass" size, "it has experienced itself as the center of events." Because of its size—which means, in part, because of its purchasing power—the generation has always been a center of attention, an experience that has bred "a certain arrogance." Davy Crockett hats and hula hoops were instant, continental fads because of this generation, the first wired, television generation. Caddell says the movie *The Big Chill*, which boomers swooned over, depicts a generation in which "pictures, remembrances, ideas and experiences are shared universally, and music is the greatest conductor of these."[21]

Were John Kennedy alive in 1988 he would be seventy-one. He and Reagan and Lyndon Johnson and Nixon and Ford and Carter came from essentially the same generation. The next President will be determined in large measure by the mood of the baby boom generation. Elections are about moods, and popular culture is a measure of moods. In the late 1970s, says Peter Hart, television foreshadowed the conservative future. Two especially popular shows were *Happy Days* and *Laverne and Shirley*. Both were set in the glow of the remembered 1950s. Peter Hart surmises that both indicated a need for reassurance. That was a Reagan specialty in the presidential election that followed, and perhaps something like it could be potent in 1988. To gauge moods Hart suggests listening to the jargon of the young. In the 1950s the young spoke of being "hep" and "cool" and "with it"—"it" denoting the right, or "in," group. The 1960s echoed with the rhetoric of "doing your own thing" and "getting your act together," a vocabulary of separateness for a decade of disintegration. Today, Hart says, the punctuating expressions of youthful discourse are "for sure" and "really"—again, a reaching for reassurance.[22]

There may be a risk in relying on the support of boomers raised on rock and roll and television. In 1984 Gary Hart's hot streak, from New Hampshire to late spring, was about as long as the run of success enjoyed by a hit record. Perhaps that is the boomers' attention span.

Music is a recurring motif in talk about the boomers. The most sensible talk distinguishes the social strata within that generation. Baby boomers are not an undifferentiated mass. And some music is said to be an index of the differentiation. In that regard, I think I have heard the future, and it is loud. What I have heard certainly is loud. It is the sound of Bruce Springsteen, and of his fans stampeding down his thunder road to snap up his latest offering. This is the sound of the future if Ralph Whitehead, a professor at the University of Massachusetts, is right about "new-collar" Americans.

Nostalgic liberals who yearn for an angry blue-collar troubadour—an electrified Woody Guthrie—and conservatives who think guitarists are all subversives hear only protest in Springsteen. True, his songs of stress, vulnerability, and precariousness are counterpoints to the "morning in America" goo of overripe Reaganism. But Whitehead says a new populism is finding a voice in Springsteen. The populism is "two parts protest to three parts affirmation."[23]

New-collar voters—the label denotes a place between blue- and white-collar—are a large component of the 78 million baby boomers. They are now two-thirds of the work force. The youngest boomers are turning twenty-two, the oldest are forty. The 25 million new-collars among them are 15 percent of the electorate.

They compromise a "community of fate,"[24] having a common array of prospects, anxieties, and aspirations. Whitehead believes that the new collars are the swing vote of the 1980s.

The other 53 million baby boomers are, presumably, blue

collar or white collar, with the relatively well-defined values, aspirations and expectations associated with those categories. The "new-collars" have a sense of vulnerability because their alternative futures could vary dramatically. They are technicians, computer operators and others in the new, post-industrial working class, which entered the work force when the manufacturing sector was stagnating and millions of jobs were emerging in the service sector. Whitehead says they are to the Eighties and Nineties what blue-collars were to the Forties and Fifties. And this is what they are not: Yuppies.[25]

The misapprehension that "Yuppie" is a synonym for "baby boomer" has had political costs. When Mondale's campaign saw that many young voters were critical of big goverment, the campaign read the criticism as rejection of the welfare state and hence of "compassion." So young people were equated with Yuppies, and Yuppies with materialism, self-absorption, and careerism. "Yuppie" became an unflattering moral concept and an inaccurate sociological category. Enter Whitehead, the man who shot the Yuppie.

Whitehead believes that quantitative measurements must be leavened by qualitative analyses of a generation's experiences, ideas, values, dreams, satisfactions, and definitions of success and failure. Most baby boomers do not feel better off than their parents economically but do feel better off in other ways. They, and especially new-collars, place high value on these other ways. Surveys indicate that baby boomers feel more able than their parents were to do interesting things, to pursue satisfaction rather than mere money in careers, freer to do what they want. Compared with Yuppies, new-collars are much more numerous, have less money and more children, and are closer to their families. Whitehead, a Democrat, has warned his party that it has in its head an anachronistic picture of the people who do America's basic work. The work has changed and so have the people.

New-collars have been shaped by the baby-boom culture. They have family incomes between $20,000 and $40,000.

They do not do the hard, dirty, physical labor of blue-collars. Rather, their work falls between traditional blue-collar work and that of upper-middle management and the professions. Whitehead makes this distinction: managers and professionals use their minds in formal, disciplined ways. Many new-collars may have attended college for a while, but they do not use their education hour by hour on the job as, say, a lawyer does.

Blue-collars tend to be fatalistic; new-collars seek control of their circumstances. Blue-collar men are disinclined toward introspection. New-collars, says Whitehead, are able and willing to talk about "states of mind and feelings." [26] They are a large portion of the prime-time television audience, and they identify with men like Frank Furillo of "Hill Street Blues," a tough guy not too reticent to reveal his hungry heart.

The new-collars cannot be defined as clearly inclined toward one party or the other. They have an interesting combination of competence and needs. Consider, for example, the fact that while blue-collars base their identities on their work, new-collars tend to base theirs on their leisure. That, and their quest for a sense of control of their work and living conditions, disposes them toward governmental activism for clean air and water, affordable homes, good schools, and security and discretion in jobs. Whitehead notes that, in the twenty-five years after World War II, government invested heavily in the new-collars' parents—the G.I. Bill to get them educated for jobs in the city, highways to get them home to houses built with VA or FHA loans in suburbs where bond issues financed schools and parks. [27]

Democrats can derive a moderate, activist-government program from the new-collars' experiences and values. Expressed in constant (1977) dollars, average weekly wages in 1985 ($170.42) were lower than in 1962 ($172.16). Median family income in 1985 was $27,735, just $399 above that of 1970 and $1,437 below the 1973 peak of $29,172. (Senator Pat

Moynihan doubts that in the nearly 400 years since Europeans settled in America there has been another 16-year period in which family income essentially did not rise.)

The rate of home ownership for people under forty-five grew rapidly during the first three decades after the war, but since 1979 the rate has been falling. In 1970 mortgage payments took 17.9 percent of the median family income; today they take 29 percent. In 1970 average annual costs of attending a four-year private university took 29.6 percent of median family income; today they take 40.4 percent.

A function of political and opinion leaders, says Whitehead, is to help people make sense of their experiences. As Reagan's presidency winds down, so will his power to interpret American life. The future may fall to those who can interpret in a political program the new-collar experiences. Recent Democratic policy pronouncements have emphasized more aid for college students, subsidized mortgages, as well as "flex-time" and "portable pensions" and day care to empower people to control more of their working lives. For Democrats these proposals could constitute a recipe for a return to the glory days that have passed them by. The principal ingredient in the recipe is recognition that government should be more of an enabler than a protector, helping people exercise choice rather than protecting them from hazards.

Peter Hart and Geoffrey Garin stress that since 1960 the proportion of high school graduates in the adult population has grown by more than 50 percent and the college-educated proportion has almost doubled. It is, therefore, not surprising that three-quarters of all new jobs created in the last quarter-century have been white-collar or sales positions. The blue-collar percentage of the work force has fallen from 40 to 25. According to Hart and Garin, this better-educated electorate feels more socially competent and less personal dependence on government.[28]

The two parties constantly vie to appear as the people's protector. Since the advent of the New Deal, Democrats have presented government programs to protect people from the vicissitudes of life. But as the electorate has become more educated and affluent, more able to protect itself, and more interested in discretionary uses of personal income than in collective purchases through government, Republican tax-cutters have come forward as protectors of the people against government.

The great engine of social change in the modern world—war—changed the average citizen's experience with taxation. It introduced the average citizen to income tax. Until World War II, fewer than 10 percent of Americans paid any federal income taxes. And in the two decades before Ronald Reagan was elected, the proportion of Americans subject to at least a 32-percent tax rate quadrupled, from one-eighth to nearly one-half.

The great event of the Democratic convention of 1984 was Walter Mondale's pledge to raise taxes to continue financing the protective state. The problem with that proposal was illustrated when a young Democratic professional called from the convention to get his father's assessment of things. The father, a blue-collar worker in the Northeast, said: "The Democratic Party has been good to me—Social Security, G.I. Bill, student loans. The Democratic Party made me middle class. But Reagan will keep me middle class."

There, neatly put, is the paradox at the heart of the Democratic party's problems. Many federal programs, most of them pioneered by Democrats, have produced a prosperous and socially competent middle-class nation that feels less need for the modern state and hence is less tolerant of the taxes needed for that state.

This paradox sometimes sends young Democratic intellectuals into flights of free-lance sociology in efforts to discover new values and variables by which Democrats can seize the imagination of the nation. So it was that in 1986 Chris Matthews, a prodigy among Democratic political operators, revved his mental motor, slapped the lever that kicks his mind into four-wheel drive, popped the clutch, and was off, explaining the Beer Commercial Theory of History.

The Democratic party, he says, has bushels of problems but its biggest is with a big group: white males. Just over 30 percent of them voted for Mondale. Now, says Matthews, gunning his imagination, most white males watch televised sports that appear in the gaps between beer commercials. The commercials show lots of blue-collar blacks and whites exuberantly drinking together in saloons. Commercial-makers know that is not the way things normally are, so what are they trying to do? Well, yes, of course: sell beer. But why the recurring image? Because (says Matthews, the needle on his intellectual tachometer bumping the edge of the dial) these integrated bar scenes are suitable accompaniments for sports, the most integrated sphere of American life. It is the sphere in which white males seek heroes. So the presidential nominees should be Jack Kemp and Bill Bradley because they have been sports heroes and can satisfy the desire for politicians who have succeeded at something besides politics.

But enough of such flights. The flat, uncarbonated truth is that American politics is a serious business. It is not about beer commercials, it is about real issues. So Democrats should learn the way football teams learn, by looking at game films. Democrats should rewind the reel of the last two decades and study their failures.

Peter De Vries, the novelist, says there is nothing like a calamity to make you forget your troubles. The calamities of 1980 and 1984 have caused many Democrats to forget that their troubles were becoming serious by the beginning of the 1970s. In 1970, as the Democratic party was sleepwalking into a decade of decline, a decade that would invigorate conservatism, the party was warned by two Democratic intellectuals. The party did not listen—or, more precisely, did not read. The warning came in a book published midway between the mayhem in Chicago in 1968 and the McGovern convention in Miami in 1972. The book was *The Real Major-*

*ity* by Richard M. Scammon and Ben J. Wattenberg,[29] two Jacksonian—"Scoop" Jackson—Democrats.

Both authors were from that portion of the party that did not turn against Lyndon Johnson. Johnson was the great implementor of post–New Deal liberalism. Regarding race, especially, he was the most achieving President since Lincoln. On a range of domestic issues he advanced, in a time of national prosperity, a program of distributive justice comparable in range to the program FDR put forward in a national economic crisis. Yet the destruction of Johnson's presidency was the first significant achievement of the forces of the left that were setting the tone of and taking control of the Democratic party. The issue that brought about the destruction was, of course, Vietnam—a war begun by, rationalized by, and then abandoned by liberal intellectuals who were aides to the two Presidents, Kennedy and Johnson, who presided over American involvement.

Wattenberg worked on Lyndon Johnson's staff. Scammon took a different, gentler route to political wisdom. After the 1960 election Scoop Jackson asked him what job he would like. Scammon said he wanted to be Director of the Bureau of the Census. Scammon was, and is, longheaded. The architect's axiom—"God is in the details"—has a political analogue. Truth is in the numbers. By 1970 Scammon was armed with some truths. And imagine the intellectual disorder of the Democratic party in 1970, when Scammon and Wattenberg had to assail the party with this truth: "The great majority of the voters in America are unyoung, unpoor and unblack; they are middle-aged, middle-class, middle-minded."[30] That is still true, and there is a fourth thing the typical voter is "un-": "unpolitical."[31]

That is, they do not think about politics often and when they do they are not often passionate. They certainly do not think that politics makes a decisive difference in their lives— at least not federal politics. The plan of the local school board to close MacArthur Grammar School, the city council's decision about putting a stop sign at the intersection of Elm and Green streets—about things like that they will get hot and bothered. The federal government is generally too remote for passion. However, the average unpolitical person understands, intuitively, that the presidency is a tone-setting institution. This matters because, as Scammon and Wattenberg saw nearly two decades ago, "many Americans have begun casting their ballots along the lines of issues relatively new to the American scene." [32]

For decades the bread-and-butter issue of American politics concerned bread and butter. That is, it concerned economics—the price of bread and butter and the jobs available to enable people to pay that price. But suddenly, in the late 1960s, voters also began to array themselves in terms of what came to be known as social issues, including law-and-order, racial tensions and backlash, anti-youth sentiment, and anxieties about changing cultural, sexual and other moral values.

In a national survey in February, 1968, Gallup asked a cleverly conceived question: "Is there any area around here— that is, within a mile—where you would be afraid to walk alone at night?" The "yes" answer was 35 percent. The sex difference was stunning. Only 19 percent of men surveyed said yes. Fully 50 percent of women did. Scammon and Wattenberg rightly read this as social dynamite: "Half the husbands in America have wives who are afraid to go out at night." [33] Scammon and Wattenberg gave this withering formulation of the liberal response to this widespread anxiety: " 'Law and order' was a code phrase for racism." [34] And, "Lady, you're not really afraid of being mugged; you're a bigot." [35] As Robert D. Squier, a Democratic consultant, was to say, looking back from the 1980s, the Democratic party dissociated itself "from the idea of representative government. We did not go left, we went up." [36]

In the 1970 elections it sometimes seemed that every candidate for House and Senate seats was running for sheriff. The dominant issue was law and order. One reason for widespread anger and anxiety about disorder was television coverage of disturbances on campuses and in urban ghettos. Another was urban street crime, the increase of which was a consequence of a demographic fact. A bulge of young people was passing through American society, like a pig in a python.

That bulge also was one cause of campus unrest. Student and junior faculty populations had suddenly grown as the cohort of college-age youth expanded and, simultaneously, a college education came to be regarded as a middle-class entitlement. The first large-scale extension of the entitlement principle to higher education occurred a generation earlier, with the G.I. Bill. It gave universities an infusion of older, exceptionally serious students who had been formed by the experiences of the Depression and war. Twenty years later the second entitlement revolution in higher education did much good, but at a cost. It made higher education accessible to many young people who otherwise might not have been able to act on their serious desire for it. The cost was that it swept on to campuses many young people who found themselves there merely because of the momentum of entitlement. That is, a significant number of people were on campuses as students simply because it was now possible for them to be there, and others were in faculty jobs primarily because suddenly the academic job market had become a seller's market. Suddenly campuses had numerous ill-at-ease students and junior faculty members whose interest in and capacity for the traditional academic were marginal. For both groups, radical politics, including the politicizing of curricula, became an alternative vocation. Meanwhile, back on the mean streets of many cities, many less privileged members of the youth cohort were doing what it was altogether predictable they would do. Young men aged fifteen to twenty-two were, as usual, committing a disproportionate share of society's crimes, and there were an awful lot of those young men.

But in a few years—by the 1976 election—law and order was no longer a salient issue in the presidential, House or

Senate elections. Campuses had gone off the boil, partly because the Vietnam war (or, more precisely and importantly,
draft calls) had stopped disturbing the peace. Ghettos were
burned-over territories, not dry tinder. Street crime, which
spread an anxiety that corrodes the urbanity of cities, was
more of a problem than ever, but it was less of an issue because voters had figured out an important fact: There is precious little that federal legislation could do about it.

Voters still wanted rhetorical nods toward their anxieties;
they wanted candidates to take the slight trouble to manifest
the right attitudes. Attitudinizing was important as a sign of
sympathy and as a way of blurring the social distinction between the public and its representatives. But law and order
had stopped being an "issue," in the sense of a problem that
could be addressed with particular policies that would be
implemented, evaluated, and modified. An issue had been
transmuted by events into an important but lesser thing—a
string on the national lute, to be plucked occasionally for its
reassuring resonance.

But as the 1970s began, Scammon and Wattenberg said that
the average unyoung, unpoor, unblack—and unpolitical—
American was disturbed by crime and other social tension,
including a sense of moral dissolution. And this average voter
was saying: "I do not expect that a politician, any politician,
can make these conditions disappear overnight. I even understand that some of the problems aren't strictly political problems. But I do expect that any politician I vote for will *be on
my side*." [37]

As the 1980s end, something of the sort is happening concerning the social issues, by now referred to in the code word
"family."

Digging and delving in the Democratic party's 1986 policy
pronouncement, "New Choices in a Changing America," you
come upon this thumping affirmation: "Families matter." [38]
What is going on? A back-to-basics movement among Demo-

crats that is ominous news to Republicans. Democrats have gone out in the pasture behind the barn to practice new lines.

Since the late 1960s, many voters have doubted whether the national Democratic party shares their anxieties about a dissolution of "traditional values." The Democrats' new policy document addresses that doubt by, among other things, lavishing attention on "the family."

By the third paragraph, the document is dispensing bromides such as: "Strong, independent families are the centerpiece of Democratic domestic policy."[39] Democrats, in their new enthusiasm, may be about to pound the idea of family policy into the sort of shapeless goo they have made of the idea of civil-rights policies. For years, Democrats have been christening their favorite domestic policies (job programs, public housing, urban renewal) as civil-rights policies, in an attempt to give them momentum and insulate them from criticism. Now there is a tendency to turn family policy into another classification that does not classify—a classification that includes everything.

Tax reform, job training, aid for small—sorry, I mean "family"—farms, all are advertised as "pro-family" policies because they ease social distress, and distress is hard on families. The traditional liberal agenda can come clothed in the language of "traditional" value.

However, the Democratic document does contain serious thoughts about the changing texture and rhythms of family life.

The median income of families doubled between 1947 and 1973 but has stagnated since then, in spite of the dramatic increase in two-income families. To repeat, mortgage payments and post-secondary education consume sharply increased portions of the median family income. Home ownership and access to college are basic aspirations of middle-class families and are becoming less accessible.

And there are other new anxieties. In the average kindergarten class today, one in six of the children was born to a teen-age mother. More than 25 percent of America's families are single-parent families and 95 percent of them are headed by women. Of all mothers with school-age children, 70 percent work outside the home. When the women who today are between thirty and thirty-nine were twenty-one to thirty, only 58.3 percent had children. Today 78.2 percent do—a 40 percent increase. Many of these women are trying to continue professional careers.

The Democratic document states that, "The most common emotion associated with child-rearing is guilt—over 'not spending enough time with the kids.' "[40] The Democrats speak tentatively, promising only to "consider" promoting such measures as parental leave for childbirth, flexible work times, job sharing, and other measures to alleviate stress and guilt. These ideas may be slender reeds on which to lean a concept as large as "family policy," but they are not less persuasive than Republican claims to be simultaneously "pro-family" and "anti-government."

The matter of "family values" marched onto the political stage from the right. It was the rallying cry of people who hoped to ban abortion and remove the ban on prayer in public schools. Those were real concerns but they also came to denote, for conservatives, a general anxiety about the pace and direction of changes in social mores. By the mid-1980s Democrats had decided that middle-class anxieties about these changes were not confined to conservatives. The most illuminating aspect of the Democratic document is the care it takes to express a particular attitude, using families as the focus. This is less an attempt to promise governmental solutions to the problem than a more modest attempt to demonstrate empathy with voters who are anxious about a problem that is not submissive to political solutions. This is why the 1986 Democratic document and banalities like "families matter" matter.

The average American does not think the welfare of his or

her family depends primarily on this or that micropolicy that delivers a particular service or benefit. Rather, it depends on the success of one macropolicy: the management of economic growth. Regarding Republican mismanagement of the economy, as exemplified by the deficit, the Democratic document is a tissue of evasions. For example, in what may be the most backhanded praise in the history of politics, the document says, "Almost any combination of approaches [to deficit-cutting] is preferable to the poison pill represented by Gramm-Rudman-Hollings" across-the-board budget cuts, but Gramm-Rudman-Hollings "is preferable to no strategy at all."[41]

When Democrats find themselves hemming and hawing they fall back on the issue they are as comfortable with as Republicans are with complaints about big government. The issue is fairness. Mondale tried to make much of the unfairness of Reagan's domestic policies, and failed. He was not overscrupulous in defining his terms.

When Jim asked Tom Sawyer what a Moslem is, Tom said a Moslem is someone who is not a Presbyterian. With similar precision Democrats say that fairness is not what Reagan delivers. Mondale seemed to measure the fairness of American society solely in terms of the domestic side of the federal budget and the incidence of taxation. This strengthened the public's perception of him as too fixated on government. Anyway, in 1980 domestic spending measured in 1987 dollars was $523.4 billion. In 1984, when Mondale ran, it was $523 billion. Reasonable people can differ about the equity of spending patterns under Reagan. But it is unreasonable to imply, as Mondale did, that since 1980 the domestic budget has become something Beadle Bumble might have dreamed up to torment Oliver Twist.

Regarding taxation, reasonable persons can differ about the equities of the system as modified by Reagan's cuts. But it is unreasonable to suggest that Reagan has seriously undermined the essential progressiveness of the system. In the mid-1980s the top 10 percent of the taxpayers accounted for 50 percent of tax revenues and the bottom 50 percent paid just 10 percent.

So, part of Mondale's problem was that Reagan has not been radical. But another part of the Democratic party's problem regarding the fairness issue is that the party has a high peculiarity quotient. But, then, there is a lot of peculiarity going around as society goes around and around in pursuit of perfect fairness.

Daniel Seligman, who collects evidence of social insanity (for his "Keeping Up" column in *Fortune* magazine), asks an interesting question. New York's police department has an affirmative-action program to recruit homosexuals because (according to the notice posted in gay bars) police officers must be "representative of the community they work to serve." Seligman wonders: How will the community know the sexual orientation of the person on the beat?[42] Is this just East Coast peculiarity? Hardly.

Backward reels the mind to the San Francisco Democratic convention and its rules committee. Lord, how Democrats love rules. The late Professor Grant Gilmore of the Yale Law School writes: "In Heaven there will be no law, and the lion will lie down with the lamb. . . . In Hell there will be nothing but law, and due process will be meticulously observed." The Democrats' rules committee endorsed creation of a Fairness Commission to fine-tune the party's rules "as they relate to the full participation in the party process of . . . [all] members of the Rainbow Coalition." The rules committee stipulated:

> The Commission shall consist of at least 50 members equally divided between men and women, and shall include fair and equitable participation of Blacks, Hispanics, Native Americans, Asian/Pacifics, women and persons of all sexual preference consistent with their proportional representation in the party.

Few voters know that Democrats, in solemn assembly, do things like this. If voters knew, Democratic candidates would suffer even worse electoral rebukes. Nevertheless, the Democratic party has lost four of the last five presidential elections. It would be rash for Democrats to assume that this has nothing to do with the fact that the party has been, as the work of the rules committee suggests, a bit too peculiar for comfort. What sends its peculiarity quotient off the charts is the issue of fairness.

Sooner or later every parent must rise up and lay down the law to the children about the use of the word that parents often refer to delicately as "the F word." It is a four-letter word. It comes tripping off even very young tongues. It is a disturber of the peace. The word is "fair."

Unless that word is banned from children's vocabularies the evening meal becomes even more stressful than it inevitably is. Arguments erupt when Billy says he has been given an unfair (slightly larger than Suzy's) stalk of broccoli and Suzy says her scoop of sherbet is unfair (slightly smaller than Billy's). Bedtime becomes bedlam as Suzy, five, says it is unfair that Billy, fifteen, gets to stay up later than the age difference warrants. And breakfast brings an especially virulent outbreak of fairness-mongering when Billy and Suzy, in harmony for once, say it is unfair that they have to eat oatmeal while the kids next door are tucking into bowls of fudge-coated sugar-munchies.

Recently American society and the government that both shapes and reflects it have come to resemble a quarrelsome, elbow-throwing family that needs a vacation from itself and its fussing about fairness. And so it came to pass that an "enough already" decision was taken in the Senate in 1986 when the Finance Committee started a healthy epidemic sweeping through Congress.

The Committee took a stunning U-turn away from complexity and toward simplicity in the tax code. Of course those who praise the tax bill do so first and foremost, and incessantly, for being exquisitely "fair." But that should not obscure the fact that the bill represented a giant and salutary step back from one of the Democratic party's favorite pastimes, the practice of trying to use the tax code to fine-tune the fairness of society. Recently, the word "reform" has become a semi-synonym for "simplification," and simplicity means, in practice, a less statist approach to the pursuit of economic and social goals. So the following fact may be portentous regarding the Democratic party's re-definition of itself as the 1988 election approaches. In 1986, in all of Congress, the prime mover in tax reform was a liberal young Democratic Senator from a northeastern industrial state.

The particular complexity of the pre-reform code (the re-formed code is, of course, also complex) has been defended, often sincerely and sometimes correctly, as the servant of equity. Of course in the eyes of Congress the equitable and the political are often indistinguishable: What is useful seems awfully fair. Still, this clearly is the case: Every complexity in the existing code is a social program, an attempt to fiddle with incentives to alter behavior, direct the flow of private sector resources, and achieve desirable social outcomes. And these social programs often are effective. It is arguable that one of the most important laws ever passed in the United States is the Sixteenth Amendment (Act of October 3, 1913, CH. 16, Section II (B), 38 Stat. 166, 167). That bit of the tax code makes mortgage interest payments deductible. It was not immediately important when it was enacted as part of the original income tax law on February 25, 1913. Prior to World War II only 10 percent of the population paid income taxes, so most of those who could take immediate advantage of deductibility in the 1930s were in an affluent minority. But by 1984 homeowners constituted two-thirds of the nation's households. Furthermore, consider those tax shelters by which the rich reduce their tax liabilities. The rich invest in partnerships that build shopping centers, apartments, office buildings. The tax code has encouraged—actually subsidized—this in order to promote construction, jobs, growth. The rich have enjoyed this; but so have the construction workers' unions.

What began in 1985 as a crusade for simplicity at first produced only modest reform proposals that would have reduced a rococo tax code to a baroque code. The 1986 Finance Committee Bill was (to continue the architectural analogy) almost Bauhaus in the degree to which it dispensed with adornments.

Actually, the bill was more (pardon my language) fair. It would make market decisions more important relative to political decisions in the allocation of resources. The justice of the market is not perfect. However, it is, more often than not, preferable to a politicized system in which the allocation of wealth and opportunity is heavily influenced by government tax-code decisions that are themselves heavily influenced by the "influence industry"—the expensive, sophisticated, Washington-based lawyer-lobbyist complex that works to make government a servant of the strong.

The 1986 tax bill said fairness is not a function of endless, complicated tinkering with the tax code. Congress wanted to give the F word a rest. As New Jersey Senator Bill Bradley said, without irony, it is time to try "temperate fairness." The Finance Committee, of which he is a member, threw up its hands, threw in the towel and did tax reform his way, pulling back from the traditional use of the tax code as an instrument for micromanaging distributive justice. It decided to simplify the code, killing many benefits to pay for lower rates for individuals. The hope was that this would mean more economic decisions made for reasons other than tax advantage, and that that would enhance economic growth. Improved growth presumably will mean not perfect justice but more justice than is produced by a political auction in which society's big battalions bid for advantages from tax-code nuances written for them.

A paradox of post–New Deal politics is that "big government," meaning government regulating economic activity in order to promote equity and efficiency, has been defended by liberals as a protector of the weak but has been used by the strong. The well-heeled (which means big labor as well as big business, and big business includes agribusiness) are well represented in Washington by people skilled at bending public power to private advantage.

Because statism in the nation's economic life has been rationalized by liberals and exploited by non-liberal interests, it is fascinating that Bradley, a Democrat from a northeastern industrial state, has shaped a tax bill that is a large step back from statism.

In a symposium, *Left, Right & Baby Boom,* published by the Cato Institute, William Schneider says one Democratic problem is "the identification of the Democrats with the government and the identification of government with the establishment and the status quo." [43] Another participant in the symposium, Michael Barone, notes that "liberals have a fairly basic problem right now: no substantial bloc of voters wants a substantially larger role for government in the economy." [44]

Terry Nichols Clark notes that this trend began locally in 1974, when half of America's cities reversed or slowed the growth of expenditures. To an increasing number of Americans, "fiscal issues are now more important . . . than government-services issues." [45] Paul H. Weaver says this trend amounts to (he will suffer for this in the next life) "proto-neolibertarianism." [46] That means decreasing belief in paternalism, increasing belief in individual discretion.

The Bradleyesque tax bill, which decreases government supervision of economic choices and increases individuals' discretionary income, fits the political analysis above. And Bradley's success suggests that the Democratic party is regaining its intellectual equilibrium. Ten years ago, important Democratic circles gave respectful hearing to nonsense like the Club of Rome report, with its suggestion that "zero growth" would be beneficial. Ten years ago, the Democratic presidential nominee promised to slash U.S. defenses. Today Bradley sums up the necessary Democratic message in two words: "growth" and "strength."

Bradley says there is "a group of Democrats who are waiting for the next recession. If it comes, they've got the answer." The answer would be the usual pump-priming spending, jobs programs, etc. What Democrats must think about, Bradley says, is "governance of a prosperous society with problems." Democrats must learn to "credibly talk about growth to people making investments." [47]

In 1988 the Democratic party's credibility—that is, come to think about it, a tiresome word; "sensibleness" will do nicely —will be tested concerning three issues. One is foreign policy, with special reference to both the Reagan Doctrine in Central America and arms control. The other two telling issues will be racial policies and the Supreme Court. These two will test the Democrats' willingness to talk sense of a sort that some of their constituencies do not want to hear.

Regarding foreign policy, the Democratic party has lost touch with its own noble tradition. This is odd because the Democrats say they revere someone who was a representative of that tradition, John Kennedy. But do Democrats remember him clearly? I do not think so. And the power of the Kennedy name to fire the party's imagination is now weak and becoming more so.

Indeed, an era ended in the Democratic party on March 18, 1980, when voters in the Illinois primary sided with President Carter against Edward Kennedy, by a thumping 780,787 to 359,875 popular votes. Illinois is as close as a state can come to being a barometer for this diverse nation. It is both industrial and agricultural. It is midwestern but also both North and South: Its northernmost portion extends farther north than Cape Cod, and its southernmost portion extends farther south than Richmond. Beginning with 1920—in sev-

enteen presidential elections—it has voted with the winner
sixteen times. Its only miss was in 1976 when it preferred
Ford over Carter. But on that Tuesday in March, 1980, voters
in the Illinois primary voted more than two-to-one for an unpopular Carter rather than for Kennedy. That was the end of
the Democratic party's debilitating preoccupation with the
Kennedy brothers. It is, therefore, now time to put President
Kennedy in perspective.

The precariousness of life, for individuals and institutions,
is illustrated by the death of Kennedy and by the life of the
Democratic party since then. And much writing about him
confirms the axiom that fame is the sum misunderstandings
that accumulate around a well-known name.

Much writing is by former supporters who project on him
their evolved social perspectives, as with civil rights, or their
failures of nerve, as with Vietnam. Certainly Kennedy's career was not a call to the kind of ferment that filled the decade
after Dallas. His narrow victory, his tactical caution and his
conservative temperament produced a presidency with a
moderate agenda. He picked a Wall Street Republican, Douglas Dillon, as Treasury Secretary and pressed for a substantial
tax cut.

Although Kennedy said the torch had been passed to a new
generation, he represented less the dawning of a new era
than the closing of a superior one. From 1945 on, Americans
had ardently pursued two goals: economic growth and containment of communism. But by the mid-Sixties, there was a
weariness with the latter and a concern to correct the costs
of the former. The costs were environmental and, many persons thought, spiritual—the conformity and sacrifice of
"self-expression" in the discipline of economic dynamism.
Kennedy, with his calls for sacrifice ("Ask not . . .") and his
promise to "get America moving" in the competition of the
Cold War, was a bright flaring of the waning flame of post-war
values.

Kennedy was preoccupied with meeting America's commitments (such as to Vietnam, where he sent 16,000 Americans) and building a strong defense. He was committed to a policy of containment around the world. That was Democratic orthodoxy. The party had been the principal foe of the principal evil of our century—totalitarianism. The party was characterized by Wilson's opposition to Lenin, Roosevelt's to Hitler, Truman's to Stalin, Kennedy's to Castro, Kennedy's and Johnson's to Asian communism. Democrats defined and waged the Cold War and did it well.

Kennedy's Inaugural Address, with its call for sacrifice anywhere, anytime in the "long twilight struggle," expressed a bipartisan consensus. Today, approval of that address comes more commonly from Republicans than Democrats. William Henry says that in 1984 "Democrats had a united vision of American's past and of their heroic role in it, but they shared no sense of how that past connected to the present and future."[48] Actually, regarding foreign policy their problem was more severe than that. Their problem was that they, or at least a significant fraction of them, regarded their party's role—and it was a heroic role—in the post-war era as ignoble.

The flinty realism and longheadedness of the Truman-Acheson Cold War tradition, of which John Kennedy was a part, has been repudiated by too many Democrats and replaced by a fundamental frivolousness that is only slightly caricatured by the following quiz:

*Question:* Since detente was codified at the Nixon-Brezhnev summit in 1973, the Soviet Union has forced a nuclear alert by threatening to intervene with troops in the October, 1973, war in the Middle East (a war incited and financed by the Soviet Union); has organized and financed the destruction of the Paris accords and a U.S. ally; has intervened with Cubans and others in Angola, Ethiopia, Yemen, Cambodia, Nicaragua and El Salvador; has invaded Afghanistan; has orchestrated the crushing of Poland; has made a mockery of the Helsinki agreements; has repeatedly violated the informally agreed-to threshold test ban

treaty (although we even changed the way we measure violations, in an effort to avoid the need to make protests that would dampen detente); has tried to murder the Pope; is violating the terms of SALT II (an amazing feat, considering that SALT II is a tissue of loopholes and ambiguities); is funding and organizing terrorism worldwide; and is continuing an arms build-up unambiguously designed for political intimidation and military aggression. The first quiz question is: Why is there a "return to the Cold War"?
Answer: President Reagan gave a speech referring to the Soviet Union as an evil empire.

The frivolousness of a few liberal intellectuals regarding foreign policy is nothing new. Irving Kristol recalls the days in the 1930s and 1940s when the fifty or so thinkers loosely associated with *Partisan Review* would hotly dispute whether they should "support" the "bourgeois" governments of Britain and France against Nazi Germany. When the Soviet Union invaded Finland, these thinkers argued about whether, given that the Soviet Union was a deeply flawed workers' state but Finland was an unregenerate bourgeois state, they—these fifty thinkers, mind you—should "call upon" Finnish workers to welcome the Soviet army. Kristol says: "Having the 'right position' was what counted, not talking sense."[49]

These frivolous few were radically unlike the many thoughtful liberals who made the Democratic party the great foe of dictators before, during and after World War II. But as the war and its generation of leaders receded into history, the ratio of the frivolous to the serious rose among liberals. The frivolousness of some in the 1960s and 1970s was often especially apparent regarding the Castro regime. Paul Hollander, author of *Political Pilgrims*,[50] notes that enthusiasm for Castro in the late 1950s and the 1960s, unlike enthusiasm for the Soviet Union in the 1930s, was not a product of a social crisis. Rather, it stemmed from boredom with Ike and "conformity" and all the other horrors (as some intellectuals saw them) of the 1950s. When the larger-than-life figures of the war years were gone there was, Hollander notes, an ebbing of the heroic in the West's political life. The Democratic party was influenced by the literary left, that "herd of independent minds." The party was tainted by the herd's smug feeling of "alienation" from American contentment. By 1956—Khrushchev's denunciation of Stalin, the crushing of the Hungarian revolt—the Soviet Union had lost all ideological élan. Leftist intellectuals looking around for a new focus for their foolishness found one in Castro. The guerrilla in green fatigues was a reproach to the man in the gray flannel suit.

John Kennedy had not yet caused the word "charisma" to be part of the common currency of political chatter when Castro caused Norman Mailer to rhapsodize: ". . . you gave all of us who are alone in this country . . . some sense that there were heroes in the world. One felt life in one's overargued blood as one picked up in our newspapers the details of your voyage. . . . It was as if the ghost of Cortez had appeared in our century riding Zapata's white horse."[51] A ghost voyaging on a white horse. George McGovern found Castro "shy, sensitive."[52] Susan Sontag, the sort of cultural figure whose literary credentials were used to legitimize leftism, found that under Castro, "Cubans know a lot about spontaneity, gaiety, sensuality, and freaking out. They are not linear, desiccated creatures of print-culture."[53]

The task of properly assessing Castro has been a test that many liberals have flunked, and the most serious foreign policy conflict between the liberal and conservative parties in the 1980s has concerned the application of the Reagan Doctrine to Central America. The crux of the Reagan Doctrine is that a communist regime's domestic policies cannot be considered "in and of themselves." They are part of a seamless web of aggressive behavior, a single dynamic of aggression against captive subjects and vulnerable nations. The President believes "history has shown that democratic nations do not start wars." His assumption is that regimes respectful of fundamental personal rights will be shaped by the popular will, and hence will lack an aggressive disposition. His premise—that the popular will is generally pacific—is questionable in particular cases, such as 1914, but it is true enough.

The Reagan Doctrine is "containment plus." It is the postwar policy of containment, plus two insights. The first insight is that the original exposition of containment—by George Kennan nearly forty years ago—was too sanguine in hoping that Russian culture would mellow the Soviet regime. The second insight is that mere containment is, therefore, too passive. It is too compatible with the Brezhnev Doctrine, which holds that all Soviet gains are irreversible. Thus the Reagan Doctrine is tradition modified in the light of evidence. Yet Democrats in control of Congress have repudiated the Reagan Doctrine as it is relevant to Central America, in the form of aid to the contras.

A sufficient reason for funding the contras is independent of a belief that they can win a military victory or compel the Sandinistas to accept diplomatic cauterization of their festering infection in Central America. The reason is bleak but serious: We should support any struggle that burdens the Soviet imperial system. We fund the Afghan resistance although there is no realistic hope that Afghanistan will be anything other than integrated into the Soviet bloc. We do it to maintain a debilitating fever in the Soviet system. The contras can contribute to a better world by delaying the day when Sandinista power is consolidated and the dynamic of Stalinism turns, as it eventually must, outward.

If Congress kills aid to the contras, it will kill the last impediment to the consolidation of Sandinista Stalinism. Suppose the Sandinistas mean what they say about waging a "revolution without borders." Suppose their military and destabilizing capabilities are aimed next at Costa Rica, which is democratic and unarmed. What then? The President and opponents of his aid proposal should be specific. Perhaps the President should propose for Costa Rica the kind of guarantee

Britain gave Poland in 1939, and every Congressman and Senator should say whether he or she approves of such a pledge; and if not, why not.

It is one thing to vote against aid for the contras on the ground that the contras cannot succeed or the Sandinistas are not as dangerous as they are cracked up to be. It is something very different to vote against the contras while also flinching from answering the question, "What if the Sandinistas are that dangerous?"

Lord Salisbury said, "If you believe the doctors, nothing is wholesome; if you believe the theologians, nothing is innocent; if you believe the soldiers, nothing is safe."[54] However, it recently has seemed that if you believe the Democrats, nothing is vital.

While Democrats have been failing to define vital interests, they also have been failing in their attempt convincingly to adjust even their rhetoric in the direction of realism. Their most interesting attempt to do so came shortly before the 1986 elections, in a pronouncement from the Democratic Policy Commission.

Sweeping the horizon with an ideological telescope, the Democrats spotted "an empire in the classical sense."[55] They meant the Soviet Union. Many Democrats suffered the vapors when President Reagan referred to the "evil empire," but the Policy Commission's pronouncement was just a four-letter adjective away from sounding similar. Democrats were trying to regain credibility by turning their rhetoric toward toughness.

The Democrats' document said: "We understand that the Soviet Union poses the greatest threat to world peace and freedom."[56] That phrase "we understand" struck a plaintive note, as in "We understand, really we do, honest." The document said: "The expansion of Soviet influence continues to pose the major threat to American interests and world peace."[57] The Democrats' new tone was designed to appeal to Democrats who have strayed rightward.

However, the tone was vitiated by the substance. Having said (another of those "Really, we mean it, sincerely—honest Injuns" protestations) that "Democrats harbor no illusions about arms control"[58] and that Soviet violations "are of as great concern to us as they are to the Republican administration,"[59] the document said: "Arms control is at the top of our agenda."[60] To which assertion the apt response is: Why? Why worship at the barren altar of arms control? The arms-control "process" has been under way for nearly two decades, during which Soviet acquisition of offensive capabilities has accelerated dramatically. About 80 percent of U.S. strategic weapons are on delivery vehicles at least fifteen years old. About 75 percent of Soviet weapons are on systems no more than five years old. The asymmetry of the arms-control process inheres in the fact that, as Dr. William R. Van Cleave, Director of the Defense and Strategic Studies Program, says, "Arms are always controlled in the West." They are controlled by societal values manifested in the media, public opinion and legislative and budgetary processes. Arms control is antithetical to the *raison d'être* of the Soviet state, which is expansion of the military power on which the state is based.[61]

In 1943, with the world in flames, Walter Lippmann reflected ruefully about his tardy disillusionment with the arms-control movement of the interwar years:

> I was too weak-minded to take a stand against the exorbitant folly of the Washington Disarmament Conference. In fact, I followed the fashion, and . . . celebrated the disaster as a triumph and denounced the admirals who dared to protest. Of that episode in my life I am ashamed, all the more so because I had no excuse for not knowing better.

Lippmann's lesson about arms control was: "The disarmament movement was, as the event has shown, tragically successful in disarming the nation that believed in disarmament."[62]

People who have witnessed post-war history have even less excuse than Lippmann had for pursuing the chimera of security-through-arms-control. As long as arms control is the centerpiece of U.S.-Soviet relations, summitry will be considered the essence of foreign policy seriousness. Summits are essentially ratifying, not deliberative, occasions. Summits are defined by the presence of heads of states. They do not personally negotiate much, and least of all do they deal with the technical details that are the essence of today's arms control. But summitry is always a box-office smash in America. It always will be until a President tells this truth: The only formula for security against totalitarians is keep your powder dry—and have lots of powder.

The great question of the twentieth century is: Can democracies find the stamina to withstand the protracted challenge of the totalitarians? Time may not be on our side. Our social memory is waning with the passing of the generation that remembers the perils of the war and the rigors of the peace, especially the Soviet suppression of Eastern Europe. As Sir Michael Howard has written: "It takes only one generation of successful peacekeeping to engender the belief, among those not concerned with its mechanisms, that peace is a natural condition threatened only by those professionally involved in preparations for war."[63]

War in the modern age has pitted not armies against armies but populations against populations. However, the post-war period has been different. In the early days of the Cold War, Western nations decided to rest their security on their technological virtuosity (weapons of mass destruction and sophisticated delivery systems) rather than civic virtue (which is more expensive in money and inconvenience because it involves conventional forces and conscription). When the Soviet Union achieved its own virtuosity, populations were again engaged, but involuntarily and passively. They were hostages under the doctrine of mutual assured destruction.

Just thirty-five years ago the U.S. strategic deterrent was a fleet of medium-range B-47 bombers, which, in a crisis, would have been moved forward to bases in Europe and Morocco and other places. Few people knew and fewer cared that all U.S. nuclear weapons were stored at two bases (in Spokane, Washington, and Limestone, Maine) and that a few enemy bombs could have destroyed the U.S. retaliatory capability. There was no sense of vulnerability.

In the 1950s the United States deployed strategic-range bombers (B-52s) and medium-range ballistic missiles (Jupiter, Thor), and work was begun on submarine-launched ballistic missiles. Soon the United States had its first ICBM (intercontinental ballistic missile), the Atlas, and had a "triad," a three-legged deterrent involving land-based, sea-based and airborne strategic weapons.

Sputnik (1957) signaled a new era. The Soviet capacity to lift large payloads posed the question we have lived with since then: How can we measure and counter the threat against the capacity of our forces to survive a first strike? For years U.S. bombers were based behind radar lines that could give ample warning of attack. And U.S. ICBMs were not vulnerable: The relatively poor accuracy of Soviet missiles—they could not count on landing closer than a few miles from U.S. silos—precluded an effective attack on the silos.

For nearly three decades the United States thought in terms of deploying new technologies and then being secure for the foreseeable future. But today, with U.S. and Soviet technologies close to even, the crucial factor is the level of investment in strategic force deployments. Before SALT I the Soviet Union was spending twice as much as the United States was. Since the misnamed arms "limitation" agreement, the Soviet Union has been spending three times as much.

Believers in arms control are undaunted by the evidence of history. But they might suffer a doubt about peace-through-parchment if they turned their attention from Geneva to the Ukrainian village of Ivanichi. There, in Middle School 2, a young teacher recently died heroically when, to protect his pupils, he absorbed the blast of a grenade.

What was a grenade doing in Middle School 2? The answer, reported by Iain Elliot in the London *Times*, is relevant to the coming argument about continued compliance with SALT II.[64]

The teacher, a graduate of KGB border-guard college (think about that), had been delivering the military instruction that is a compulsory part of the curriculum for Soviet children. He was teaching how to handle what should have been an unarmed grenade. When he pulled the pin a wisp of smoke showed that a live grenade had become mixed in with demonstration grenades, and he gave his life.

The children's manual, which teaches "hatred for the enemies of socialism," also teaches assembly of machine guns and the use of bayonets and rifle butts in the "decisive armed conflict of the two opposing world systems," a conflict that will involve "vast casualties on an unprecedented scale." As Elliot says, "The soldiers now carrying out orders and committing atrocities in Afghanistan began playing serious war games with their first steps in education."[65]

It is with representatives of this manic militarism that U.S. officials are planning to negotiate substantial reductions of offensive strategic-force levels. The promise that such reductions would come in SALT II was what made SALT I's high and unequal limits, and the ABM Treaty, palatable to Congress in 1972. But Soviet deployments of offensive systems accelerated, as reasonable people expected from a nation that teaches children to handle grenades.

Communist regimes have been stains on the planet for seventy years and never has one been talked down from totalitarianism to pluralism. The Soviet regime is the only regime among those aligned with Hitler at the beginning of World War II that has survived without a rupture. And in the late 1980s this is the paralyzing paradox of Soviet society. It is supposed to be a collectivist society ruled by "science" rather than individualist interests. Yet the interests of the individuals in the ruling class require the pretense of a "science" of progress that is the basis of that class's claim to privileges.

It has been said that the problems confronting the industrialized democracies are solvable by policy changes, whereas Soviet problems require systemic changes. Nothing announced or even foreshadowed by Gorbachev's first years suggests such change. So the Soviet crisis of congealment will continue, and the Soviet Union will become decreasingly suited to the modern world.

Pat Moynihan says the delicate U.S. task is "managing the decline" of the Soviet Union. "For as they come to sense they are doomed, they must become ever more dangerous"[66] Henry Rowen of the Hoover Institution, writing in an article entitled "Living with a Sick Bear," said the interest of the West is in "letting the Soviet system decay."[67] He argues that Soviet "economic sickness, as opposed to negotiations on arms, is a much more promising path to achieving an improvement in our security."[68]

The Soviet Union has passed the apogee of its doomed attempt to keep pace with the West. As the world becomes more complicated and evolves more rapidly, it requires of societies fluidity, adaptability and other prodigies of freedom. The Soviet Union will see the gap between it and the democracies widen—if the democracies keep their nerve and keep the pressure on.

One Soviet strategy will be the combination of parasitism and cynicism known as detente: more subsidized trade with the West, more purchases of technology, more espionage, more anesthetizing of Western publics. The West may think, yet again, that detente, which the Soviet regime desires as an alternative to systemic change, will stimulate such change. Or, the West may offer detente to assuage Soviet desperation that could result in a lunge for supremacy through aggression.

The sensible way to respond to Soviet decline is by hastening it. Policy should be: No detente, and more of the Reagan Doctrine of increasing the cost of the Soviet empire by supporting insurrections at the margins of the empire (Afghanistan, Nicaragua, Angola). The Soviet Union is no longer (in Churchill's words, October 1939) a riddle wrapped in a mystery inside an enigma. It is conspicuously an invalid trapped in a bureaucracy drunk on a nineteenth-century fallacy, Marxism. It is a system being driven toward suffocation and anemia, its deserved destinations.

Only foolish Western policies—too little defense spending, too much subsidized trade, too few restrictions on industrial espionage and technology transfers—can save the Soviet Union from steady decline. Unfortunately, commercial democracies are prone to such policies. The Democratic party, by its recent record on foreign policy, has acquired a burden of proof. It must prove that it has reacquired the realism of the Truman-Acheson era in which the Democratic party saved the West.

Now consider a domestic issue. Regarding race, the second issue that will test the sensibleness of the Democratic party in 1988, the question is similar to the one confronting the party about foreign policy. The question is: Can the party reestablish contact with some of its recently abandoned convictions?

The courage to face, and speak, unpleasant truths is the special duty of the Democratic party regarding race. It is the party that has the confidence of black Americans. It must demonstrate a capacity to say things that its most loyal constituency does not enjoy hearing. This the Democratic party has conspicuously flinched from doing. Instead it has gone about the bad business of betraying the great ideal of the original civil rights movement, a color-blind society.

Scampering, like cats on hot bricks, from one euphemism to another, the Democratic party has settled on "compensatory opportunity" the (language of the 1976 platform) and "race-conscious remedies" and "goals"—never, ever say "quotas"—to blur the outlines of what it has done. What it has done is commit apostasy. It has abandoned the quest for a society in which race is an impermissible basis for state action. Liberal defenders of reverse discrimination say it is necessary during this "transitional" period of dealing with consequences of slavery, racism, sexism, etc. But racial entitlements, once established, will be, like most such programs, immortal. The beneficiaries, including the administrators, of the racial and sexual spoils system will never say—on the basis of what criteria would they say?—that the consequences of racism, sexism, etc., have been corrected.

The candidacy of Jesse Jackson is a natural consequence of all this. Jackson is a dash of ginger in American politics, a spice, not a nutriment. In 1984 *The New Republic* said Jackson's candidacy was another badge of black isolation and was threatening the dream that made it possible: the dream of a nation no longer obsessed with race. It said Jackson has no experience building interracial coalitions and practices a politics that depends on keeping blacks separate as a bargaining unit. He offers "a vision of democracy as a spoils system, of rhetoric as arousal without persuasion, of politics as an exercise in the cultivation of false hopes, and of policy as sterile, marginal posturing beyond the fringes of the national consensus." [69]

And in recent years there has been another related but unlovely spectacle. It is white lawyers and editorial writers telling blue-collar whites that promotions or jobs or seniority systems must be sacrificed in the name of racial reparations. It calls to mind Artemus Ward's jest during the Civil War: "I have already given two cousins to the war, and I stand prepared to sacrifice my wife's brother rather than that the rebellion be not crushed."

The acid of "race conscious" policies has been seeping into the law, eroding a bedrock principle of this Republic, the

principle that rights inhere in individuals, not groups. By as-
signing privileges based on race or sex, government incul-
cates the habit of thinking of individuals as deriving their
dignity and social weight from membership in particular
groups. Government has been drawn into the odious business
of delineating the qualities—what percentage of Negro
blood, what degree of Spanish-speaking skill—that constitute
membership in a government-approved minority.

Most black leaders of the old civil-rights groups now deny
the principle that once animated those groups. It is the principle that race should be irrelevant to civic life and is inherently unacceptable as a basis for state action. These leaders
have a vested interest in expanding what has emerged in the
name of affirmative action: a racial spoils system of hiring
quotas, minority "set asides" and the rest. Such leaders denounce blacks who deviate from the old orthodoxy that government action is the key to improving the condition of
blacks.

Blacks especially, but all Americans, too, suffer from the
shortage of black leaders, especially elected leaders who will
say this: The principle impediment to the improvement of
blacks' lives is not racism; and changes in behavior of individuals can do more than changes in government policy.

Those two propositions are true, as is this: Blacks in metropolitan ghettos face economic and cultural problems that
would not be significantly less daunting were the blacks to
become white.

Nothing does more to perpetuate poverty than the disintegration of black families, and especially the conceiving of
children out of wedlock. When two-thirds of the children
born in a ghetto are illegitimate, that is a catastrophe that is
not the fault of "society" and cannot be corrected by Congress. Glenn C. Loury, a black professor at Harvard's Kennedy School notes that we live in the "post-civil-rights" era.
The principal challenge is the "internal problems which

lower-class blacks now face."[70] The problems are internal in the sense that they "involve at their core the values, attitudes and behaviors of individual blacks."[71]

In 1938 major-league baseball was white and the back of the bus was black. Nothing finer can be said of the last fifty years than that in 1988 our children consider such social practices as bizarre and distant as we consider medieval medicine. In 1938 the problem of race was thought to be a problem of extending formal rights, especially the franchise. In 1988 we know that the task of enhancing equality of opportunity is staggeringly more complicated than that.

For generations the liberal agenda had two kinds of components. One was the extension of formal rights—to labor in the 1930s, to blacks in the 1960s. The second was the expansion of entitlements to social insurance (Social Security, Medicare, etc.). Today no group comparable to labor or blacks lacks formal rights, and there are insufficient revenues for existing social programs, let alone for some large addition to the welfare state, such as national health insurance. Much remains to be done for blacks, from early intervention (prenatal care, infant nutrition) through adult training. But this is a complex agenda, not easily comprehended or quickly fruitful, so it is of limited political utility.

However, the fundamental political problem is a failure of political nerve. Political discourse has been impoverished by a black leadership class reluctant to focus on the values, attitudes and behavior of individuals, and by white politicians who pander to black leaders by following those leaders' example. Because the Democratic party has the loyalty of blacks, it must now get their attention with straight talk about the limited relevance of government action to the problems of the black underclass. Unfortunately, Democratic candidates are reluctant to talk tough sense to blacks because the black vote can be crucial in the nomination contest.

Only fourteen congressional districts (three are in Chicago) have black voting-age majorities. But blacks comprise at least

20 percent of the population in eighty-four districts that may be decisive in Democratic primaries. All but twenty-three are in the South. (And Reagan carried most of the twenty-three, so heavily are white Southerners voting Republican.) Fifty-three percent of all blacks live in the South. But in four of the five states with the most electoral votes (California, New York, Texas, Illinois—a total of 136 electoral votes, just more than half of the 270 needed to win), there are more than a million black voters. Twenty-eight of the nation's largest cities have more than 100,000 blacks. In twenty-four of the twenty-five largest school systems, a majority of the students are black or other racial minorities.

In six electorally crucial northern industrial states, Illinois, Michigan, New Jersey, New York, Ohio and Pennsylvania, there are approximately 5.5 million blacks of voting age—a lot of them hitherto unregistered.

Forty years ago 40 percent of blacks still identified with the GOP, "Lincoln's party." But forty years ago, at the Democratic convention in Philadelphia, the young mayor of Minneapolis, Hubert Humphrey, issued a clarion call for his party to seize the day regarding civil rights. The call was considered so recklessly radical by some Democrats that it produced Strom Thurmond's Dixiecrat campaign that year. In 1956 Adlai Stevenson got only 61 percent of the black vote. In 1960 John Kennedy received only 68 percent of the black vote. I say "only" because if Republican presidential candidates today received, as Nixon did in 1960, 32 percent of the black vote, Republicans would virtually own the White House.

The crucial year was 1964, the year the GOP nominated Goldwater, who voted against that year's Civil Rights Act. Lyndon Johnson won 94 percent of the black vote. Between 1960 and 1964 the percentage of blacks who identified themselves as Democrats jumped from 53 to 80. Since 1964 no Democratic presidential candidate has received less than 85 percent of the black vote.

A paper prepared by Thomas E. Cavanagh of the Joint Center for Political Studies, a black research organization, notes that three events turned blacks into the Democratic party's most cohesive block. One was the relief provided by the New Deal. Another was Harry Truman's civil rights legislation. The third was the Republican's nomination of Goldwater. The paper, written in 1984, says, "Not only are poor blacks dependent on government transfer programs, the black middle class is also heavily reliant on the public sector for employment opportunities and contracting arrangements."[72] This limits the extent to which the GOP can appeal to blacks even if it invigorates the private sector.

Since the civil-rights revolution, the Democrats' share of the black vote has been: 1968, 85 percent; 1972, 87 percent; 1976, 85 percent; 1980, 86 percent. Note that last figure. Jimmy Carter got all but 14 percent of the black vote and lost all but six states. In 1980 Carter carried seven entities—six states and the District of Columbia. Two of them, the District and Hawaii, have non-white majorities. Two of them, the District and Maryland, have large numbers of the only other group, aside from blacks, that votes solidly Democratic—government workers.

The wonder is that Democrats won anything in 1980, considering their intra-party zaniness. At the convention, Puerto Rico had more votes (41) than Oregon (39) or West Virginia (35). California's Democratic party reserved 15 percent of its delegate slots for Hispanics—then counted Greeks as Hispanics. Michigan's liberal Democratic leadership, alarmed by the George Wallace victory in the 1972 primary, limited the 1980 electorate to party activists, who were notably liberal. Thus, only 1,648 participated in the caucuses. In 1980 forty-six million people—one-fifth of the nation—were members of minorities entitled to special treatment. Within the Democratic party, this is what started in 1965: Lyndon B. Johnson said, "We seek . . . not just equality as a right and a theory, but equality as a fact and equality as a result."[73]

Other than Lyndon Johnson, who ran in the aftermath of an assassination and against a self-destructive opponent, no Democrat since Roosevelt has received a majority of the white vote. So the Democratic party is now in its fifth decade without such a majority. There is a connection between that fact and the fact that the Democratic party has itself become Balkanized. Samuel P. Huntington ascribes some of the Democratic party's disorientation to the doctrine of "categorical representation,"[74] the theory that the interests of particular groups can be properly represented only by members of those groups. That thought is now codified in the Democratic party's quota systems. The Democratic party has swallowed a large dose of the medicine it has prescribed for the country, and it has found the medicine toxic. In response we should say, in our best bedside manner: "Serves you right." The Democratic party should give itself, and the country, a respite from such remedies.

In 1988 there will be a third telling test of the Democratic party's intellectual honesty and willingness to talk sense about matters that stir hot passions. The test will come when Democrats turn, as turn they surely shall, to the subject of our most intellectually demanding institution, the Supreme Court.

In 1988 Democrats will make much of a fact that indeed should loom large in the minds of voters. It is the fact that on January 1, 1988, five members of the Supreme Court will have an average age of seventy-five. The question is, which party should superintend the coming transformation of the Court?

It is said that only God can change the Court. But George Washington, who was, so to speak, present at Creation, nominated thirteen Justices in an era when the Court only had six members. FDR, who served eleven years, nominated nine Justices—eight in four years (1937–1941). Jackson nominated seven, Taft six, Lincoln and Eisenhower five. Carter was the only President to serve a full four-year term without filling an opening on the Court. Of the 103 Justices who have served on the Court, 33 served twenty years or longer. Roger Taney was still Chief Justice when he died at eighty-seven in 1864. Louis Brandeis retired at eighty-two, Hugo Black at eighty-five, Oliver Wendell Holmes at ninety. More Justices have died in office than have retired.

The next President will find the Court closely divided and will have a chance decisively to tip the balance. There is nothing wrong with the parties, or the candidates, talking about their intentions regarding appointments to the Supreme Court or the federal judiciary generally. Indeed, given the grotesque and increasing importance of courts in national policy-making, it would be a dereliction of duty for the parties and candidates not to be forthcoming about their intentions. However, given the recent record of liberalism's recourse to courts, it may be difficult for Democrats to convince the country that they are the best custodians of the courts.

The judicial branch is an aristocratic and hierarchical branch grafted onto a democratic tree. It is an arena of close reasoning about technical matters that are hard for the public to comprehend. Furthermore, in our wired nation the public has a shrinking attention span. People are comfortable only with communication served up in brief visual bursts. So the public finds courts, where the written word reigns, increasingly alien.

Liberals have become too familiar with courts. When political movements become anemic, they abandon legislation for litigation, using courts as shortcuts around democratic processes. Conservative opponents of the New Deal did that. Today, liberals do that regarding abortion, capital punishment, race, environment, women's issues and other matters. As liberalism became lazy and arrogant, and then weak and unpopular, it retreated from political arenas to courts. There it now is besieged—and disarmed. Having won most of its recent political victories (on race, abortion, capital punish-

ment) in courts, it cannot convincingly decry the "politicizing" of courts.

A cliché more frequently uttered than demonstrated is that
the Supreme Court follows election returns. Actually, sometimes election returns respond to the Court. The electorate's
recent rightward movement may have been in part a reaction
against Court decisions considered triumphs of ideology over
reasonableness, and manifestations of a Washington impulse
to fine-tune society.

Liberal judicial activism has not been justified by any explanation as crude as "following election returns." Rather, it
is rationalized as a way of correcting the "infirmities" of representative institutions and the "timidities" of elected officials by addressing "unmet social needs." But this principle
is a close cousin to another one: Courts should take their
bearings from social judgments and political outcomes. However, jurisprudence should not be result-oriented. It should
emphasize process and the duty of judges to render decisions
controlled by the text, history and structure of the law.

Abortion is the issue most likely to galvanize interest in the
composition of the Supreme Court. Regarding abortion, a distinction must be drawn between two considerations, one political and the other constitutional. The question of whether,
or how, abortion should be regulated is political, meaning a
question about the allocation of important social values. But
there also is the question of whether the 1973 Supreme Court
decision, and those decisions that have flowed therefrom,
represent a reasonable reading of the Constitution. Both are
questions about which honorable and intelligent people of
good will can and do disagree. That is fine. Let us argue.

What is not fine is the attempt made by many Democrats to
say that the constitutional question cannot be reargued, and
that raising it is a breach of constitutional etiquette. That idea
at least, and at best, rests on a serious misconception about
the ethics of constitutional controversy. But there also is cyn-

icism mixed with ignorance in the manufactured indignation about attempts to get the Court to reconsider its rulings regarding abortion. The indignation is designed to stigmatize as dishonorable any attempt to alter the Court's course.

Liberalism's path into the wilderness has been paved with such ideological quirkiness, such ignorance and disingenuousness, such disregarding of large facts of American history. Have liberals forgotten that the civil-rights movement was a campaign to reverse the Court, especially the "separate but equal" doctrine? Furthermore, America's noblest political career was ignited by, and built around, a determination to undo the Court's decision concerning Dred Scott. Supporters of that decision thought it would end the controversy about slavery. Lincoln thought it should not. The transcript of his July 10, 1858, speech reads:

> Somebody has to reverse that decision, since it is made, and we mean to reverse it, and we mean to do it peaceably. . . . The sacredness that Judge [Stephen] Douglas throws around this decision, is a degree of sacredness that has never been before thrown around any other decision. . . . It is an astonisher in legal history. [*Laughter*] It is a new wonder of the world. [*Laughter and applause*] [75]

Some of today's misreading of American history is tendentious, intended to have a chilling effect on public discussion by shrinking the agenda of discussable policies. But some of the misreading is honest ignorance. Some people are so busy defending "the American way" that they will not take time to acquaint themselves with even the central themes and great careers of the American story.

The Court, more than any other American institution, depends, for its authority, on the perception of it as a place where principle reigns. Judicial review is somewhat anomalous in a system of popular government, and its legitimacy depends on the belief that those who exercise it do so only as construers of the text and structure of a document that allocates powers primarily to other institutions. That belief cannot withstand a selection process that suggests that Justices somehow represent this or that group interest. It is now especially important to insist on that point because of what has become the rhythm of America's welfare state.

Congress enacts an entitlement program in which crucial terms are, inevitably, somewhat undefined. During hearings and debates, Congressmen and Senators naturally express themselves generously regarding what they hope the law will accomplish. Later, activists look for promising cases to litigate, hoping that courts will construe the legislators' expressed hopes as the implied legislative intent. Then when a court defines a practical limit of Congress' intent, activists know where they need to seek to enrich the act in a second effort in Congress or in litigation involving different particulars.

The judicial branch is clogged because Americans believe that every social issue can be cast as a conflict of individual rights and that every dispute can and should be adjudicated. The legislative and executive branches also reflect the tangled moods of the populace: the instant desire for omniprovident government, and the equally strong resentment about the cost of that. The most dismaying fact about the U.S. government today is that it is indeed what it is designed to be: representative. It represents the country's conflicting desires. And both parties are wary about the risks involved in trying to accommodate those desires.

The GOP still has somewhat the mentality of an opposition party. It has been said that the function of conservatism is to extract the truth contained in each succeeding heresy. That is an appropriately modest task for a political philosophy that turns on prudence. Since 1945, Republicans have performed it by accepting the premises, and resisting the excesses, of the post–New Deal role of government.

They have accepted the federal responsibility for civil

rights (understood as access to political and economic opportunity), but have resisted "race-conscious" policies such as group entitlements. Republicans have accepted federal responsibility for the economy's performance, but have tempered liberal confidence in fine-tuning through demand-management. Republicans have accepted federal responsibility for a welfare "social minimum," but have punctured excessive confidence in government's ameliorative powers.

The conservative party's President has done what serious leaders do: He has forcefully put questions to the country. But he has not received exactly the answers he wanted. To the question: "What sort of federal role do you want?" the country has answered: "About what we have—no more, but not much less, either." Now conservatism's task is to come to terms with that answer, and finance it.

The Democratic party's task is more complicated. Michael Barone argues that the Democrats' predicament derives not from failure but from phenomenal successes. For 40 years Democrats and their ideas prevailed in almost every political battle:

> In 1930 most Americans did not believe that the federal government had a responsibility to maintain a strong economy with low unemployment and to provide sustenance for those who could not find it for themselves; by 1964 most Americans did. In 1930 most Americans did not believe that the federal government should guarantee the civil rights of blacks; by 1970 most Americans did. Democrats have, in effect, written the history books: most Americans believe that Franklin Roosevelt was a good president and Richard Nixon a bad one, and they believe that John Kennedy was the best of all. They believe that isolationism before World War II was wrong and they believe that the Vietnam war was wrong too.
>
> On the surface the political dialogue of the 1980s seems dominated by conservatives, people who call for less domestic spending, a stronger defense, lower taxes, and less government interference in business. But just beneath that

surface dialogue are values that represent a liberal consensus. Voters want government spending controlled, in the abstract; but they also want continuation of just about every specific government spending program they can think of. They want a tougher foreign policy, but after Vietnam they are hesitant indeed to risk any American military involvement abroad.[76]

The public is confused. So, understandably, are the parties. Republicans are in a somewhat sour mood as they come to terms with the fact that this "conservative era" rests on what Barone rightly identifies as a liberal consensus. And Democrats, who have won most of the major policy arguments of the post-war period, have been losing their potency in the competition for the great prize of American politics, the presidency. It just does not seem . . . fair.

In their recent confusion many Democrats have substituted moral arrogance for intellectual rigor, evidently hoping that guilt-mongering and moral blackmail can be the ingredients of a successful electoral appeal. Well, even the most formidable persons have weaknesses. Achilles had his heel. Othello was prone to jealousy. And many Democrats have been telling people one thing that everyone knows is false: that the choices confronting government are easy for the morally upright.

There hangs about the Democratic party an aura of moral overreaching. A symptom is the use of words like "decent" and "sane," as in "a decent society requires" this or that, and "we propose a sane arms-control policy." And what is the uproar about? Washington's principal industry, the indignation industry, is going to slip a disk if it keeps on straining to argue that the nineteenth century has been reinstalled by Reagan—whose fiscal 1987 budget allocated two-and-a-half times more, in real terms, for programs for low-income persons than was spent in 1970.

Today there are 5 million more persons receiving food stamps than received them during the worst of the 1975 recession. Reagan is spending almost as much on the elderly ($17,060 per couple) as on defense. Maybe more domestic spending is needed and would be prudent. But it is silly to say that the domestic budget, which is roughly the same as the 1980 spending level, represents a clash of fundamental principles with Democrats concerning federal responsibilities.

Yet, on election eve, Mondale told a crowd that Republicans never use the word "decent." Democrats would do well to quit using it. Mondale frequently said, "I would rather lose an election about decency than win one about self-interest." Such rhetoric, implying that Republicans are not just wrong but indecent, is the extreme moralizing of a party out of the habit of thinking and even arguing, and in the habit of asserting a moral monopoly.

It ought to be possible for politicians to call attention to problems without, in the process, seeming to disparage the public's moral sensibilities and to celebrate their own. However, from the left and the right we are being bombarded by the rhetoric of people whom Joseph Epstein calls "virtucrats."[77] They are people who, no matter what else they say, always say "I'm fundamentally a damn fine person." Epstein, editor of The American Scholar, says the virtucrat is a "modern Diogenes who, in search of one good man, knocked off after turning his lantern on himself."[78]

Epstein says that "anti-war" and "pro-life" are labels of virtucratic self-advertising, announcing that the holder of the particular political views is large-hearted and great-souled and obviously is opposed by people who are not just wrong, they are next door to depraved.[79]

Today the right wing has its share of virtucrats of the "when Jesus returns he will register Republican" sort. But Epstein says virtucrats are found more frequently on the left. People on the left, he says, seem to need to feel they are good-hearted, whereas conservatives are content to feel they are obviously correct.[80] Disagree with a conservative and he will call you dense. Disagree with a liberal and he will call you selfish, insensitive and uncompassionate. Liberal virtucrats decorate their Volvos with bumper stickers that say, "You can't hug a kid with nuclear arms,"[81] a thought the policy connotations of which are unclear, but which clearly says: The driver of this car is an admirably caring person.

Honk if you wish such people would go away. If they will not go away, perhaps they will take a tip from John Updike. He has his fictitious novelist, Henry Bech, receive the Melville Medal, "awarded every five years to that American author who has maintained the most meaningful silence."[82]

Of course silence is not permitted in politics, so in 1988 Democrats should try to adopt a tactic used by a dark horse Republican candidate during 1987.

Shortly after 1984, Pierre Du Pont sent out to seek "damn right" issues. He said: "What Ronald Reagan said to the country in 1980 is that communists are bad, taxes are too high, defenses are too weak and I'm going to get government off your backs. Every guy on a tractor or in a coffee shop could listen to that and say, 'Damn right.' "[83] Of course Reagan has not got government off American backs—whatever doing so might mean—but that does not matter much because that promise was yesterday's trigger for the "damn right" reflex of the folks in the coffee shops. For 1988 new triggers are needed.

For his part, Du Pont spent 1987 telling high schoolers he favored random drug testing of students, beginning at age thirteen, with this bone-chilling sanction: Those testing positive cannot get drivers' licenses until two years after they would otherwise be eligible. He said he would require all able-bodied welfare recipients, other than those with infants under, say, one year old, to work, either in the private sector or for government at 90 percent of the minimum wage, with health and day-care programs. "Mothers on welfare don't face any different problems in going to work than working mothers." He said he would require mendicant nations of the

Third World to work more rationally. That is, he would make aid contingent upon movement toward lower taxes, fewer subsidies, freer markets. "They have to admit socialism doesn't work." (What's that you just said? "Damn right"?)

What are liberal "damn right" issues? I do not know. But some Democrats think they have found one in protectionism.

The trade problem is widely perceived to be, in large measure, a problem with the Japanese. They are considered guilty until proven innocent of "unfair" practices such as erecting non-tariff barriers (often maddening bureaucratic impediments to U.S. exports) and "dumping" their exports in U.S. markets. The presumption of guilt is reasonable. The Japanese have been aggressive to a fault, tricky, obdurate, disingenuous and, most infuriating of all, successful. Their successes have cost many American jobs. But Japan's successes in the American market have pleased scores of millions of American consumers. It would be hard to find an American household that has not contributed to the "trade problem" by buying Japanese goods. Yet Americans by the millions sit in front of Japanese television sets saying "damn right" when the newscast includes a "sound bite" of a politician proclaiming that something must be done about the trade imbalance.

And consider another paradox. Protectionism is supposed to be a product of hard times. When sluggish growth causes unemployment to rise, you expect a rising desire to fend off foreign competition. So why is protectionist sentiment reaching a rolling boil in an America that has experienced half a decade of sustained growth? There may be many contributing factors, but one thought deserves special consideration because it teaches this timely and cautionary lesson: Economic categories can carry you only so far, even when the subject is economic.

Start with an economic fact, indeed a megafact: The U.S. budget deficit is larger than the GNPs of 158 of the world's 167 nations. It drives up government borrowing, which helps explain why today's real interest rates are high. Those rates helped drive up the dollar, which made imports even cheaper, until the Reagan administration set about driving the dollar down. But there is more to the explanation of today's protectionism, as expressed in Japan-bashing, than the logic of exchange rates. There also is the illogic of certain consumption.

Suppose, says Pat Moynihan, that all the hydrochloric acid used in America were imported. Who would care? But cars are a different kind of commodity, at least for Americans. Historian Daniel J. Boorstin explains why. In America, as elsewhere, consumer goods can be objects of envy and hence causes of social divisions. But in America certain consumption goods became sources of communitarian sentiment. At times, Boorstin says, Americans have acquired a sense of affiliation less by what they believe than by what they consume. People who never knew one another became members of consumption communities, joined by their use of quite similar products.

Two years ago a college graduating class was subjected to a cultural rarity, an interesting commencement address. In it Moynihan, employing Boorstin's insight, prophesied what has since come to pass—an anxiety that gives rise to protectionism. Automobiles and TV sets are, Moynihan said, the two most-used artifacts in American life. And suddenly an unsettling number of them are not American. This has rubbed raw a national nerve: Wherever Americans look, across the highway or the living room, there are physical intimations that Americans are losing their ability to compete.

Protectionism may be related to the consumers' frayed psyches, but it certainly is one form of a familiar, recurring reflex of government, a reflex that Democrats seem particularly disinclined to resist. It is the reflex to protect organized, intense client groups from change.

American history is a history of unprecedented change— social, political, commercial, technological, intellectual—

without supervision by state power. State power has been of secondary, even tertiary, importance to the intellectual and scientific forces that have transformed the twentieth century. And, to repeat, in this optimistic country, change means hope. Liberalism lost its grip on the country when it built a government that showered benefits on client groups that then had a stake in the status quo. Such liberalism made the Democratic party the party of government and government's clients (principally, public employees and the poor).

So in 1984, of the nation's twenty-five largest metropolitan areas, twenty voted for Reagan. Mondale's five were: home (Minneapolis–St. Paul), the one with the highest unemployment (Pittsburgh), the symbol of rust-belt distress (Cleveland), the host of the Democratic convention (San Francisco), and the home of bureaucracy (Washington). However, Mondale did well with another set of twenty-five cities. He carried twenty of the twenty-five that lost population in the 1970s. That is understandable. People who are in distress because change has come to seem menacing are apt to support the party that promises more ameliorative government.

Now, there is nothing inherently wrong with ameliorative action from government. However, because the instinct of modern government, and especially of liberal administrations, is to protect all client groups from all discomforts of change, modern governments often are reactionary. They react against change. And they are schizophrenic reactionaries: They divide their energies between fostering economic dynamism and resisting the logic of dynamism. In 1885 most Americans were in farming. Today about 3 percent are, and they are so prodigiously productive that we still have too many farmers. If the market is allowed to weed out the weak, the strong will prevail and the rest will be moved on to other productive employment. Recently one-quarter of all savings-and-loan institutions went under during the shakeout stimulated by deregulation. One-quarter of all jobs in the auto industry disappeared as the industry became leaner and more productive. Half of all steelworkers lost their jobs. Vigorous capitalism constantly has such disinvestments. Economic rationality produces pain. No pain, no gain.

The developed democracies today have different national characters but have this in common: Their governments have moved steadily away from being the administrators of orderly markets and toward an increasingly active redistributive role, supplanting markets as allocators of wealth and opportunity. This role generates inflationary pressures as government distributes benefits faster than productivity grows to pay for them. This, in turn, sets politicians to dreaming of a "social contract" that would bring society's factions together in the political system.

But the government behavior that makes this desirable also makes it impossible. Government—omnipresent, omniprovident and hyperactive—has ceased to be seen as a unifying agency. Rather it is seen as the object of contention, the focus of a struggle of all against all, a public prize to be captured for private purposes. A "social contract" to restrain the increasingly political and fierce struggle over shares of the national product presupposes considerable social cohesion, the absence of which is at the heart of the problem the "social contract" is supposed to solve.

Europeans often identify labor unions as the principal obstacles to an economically efficient "balance of social power." But the primary obstacle to a "balance of social power," in America as in Europe, is the politicization of the economy, which has raised the stakes of politics and the tempers of the electorates.

One theory bruited about in the 1970s was that nations could tame their domestic economic problems, and help developing nations in the bargain, by practicing the "ethics of renunciation"—that is, by slowing growth and reducing their claims on the world's resources. That theory is dead, killed by this fact: The publics in all industrial democracies have made promises to themselves, through their welfare state mechanisms, that they cannot fulfill unless economic growth is steady and rapid.

As stable societies mature, they become like long-simmered stews, viscous and lumpy with organizations resistant to change and hence inimical to economic dynamism. Democracy becomes a means for such old interests to promote policies that protect those interests but retard growth. A frequently neglected task of government is to lengthen society's time horizon. But government is constantly driven to preserve the status quo. So, for example, an institution designed to allocate capital to tomorrow's "winning" industries (such an institution is usually proposed in connection with an "industrial policy") is apt to be diverted to practicing "lemon socialism," bailing out Chryslers that already have constituencies.

Many industrial societies have been bedeviled by the inescapable tension between two goals, raising collective prosperity (which means growth, which means dynamism and some casualties) and enhancing individual security. For several generations most citizens of most industrial democracies were enthusiastic about, and most others were reconciled to, a ratchet effect whereby government measures to enhance security frequently expanded and never contracted. The election of Margaret Thatcher in 1979 and Ronald Reagan in 1980 signaled, if not a desire to reverse the ratchet, at least a desire for a pause to assess the trend.

Stable societies accumulate interest groups capable of using political power to institutionalize protections and other privileges. These groups have a growing stake in the status quo. One purpose of political leadership should be to reconcile stable societies to what Pete Du Pont calls "reinvigoration from within" through the wholesome disruptions inflicted by economic growth.

The great argument of 1988 will be a new installment in America's oldest argument. William Schneider writes:

The role of government is the eternal issue in American politics. An economically activist federal government is one that manages, guides and regulates the economy. Is that liberal or conservative? In the nineteenth century, when government was regarded as a bastion of privilege, the out-groups of society favored a *laissez-faire* state. Jacksonian Democrats, as the party of the "left," opposed many forms of government economic intervention, such as a national bank, incorporation through legislative charter, and even government-sponsored internal improvements. The Federalists, the Whigs, and later the Radical Republicans were more comfortable with statism and government intervention (for instance, Henry Clay's "American System"), which they defended in the name of nationalism.[84]

Both parties are participating in a debate that was raging nearly 200 years ago when Alexander Hamilton wrote his "Report on Manufacturers" and Jeffersonians dissented from his vision of government active in promoting commercial vigor. Then as now, Americans were trying to define the appropriate government response to the fact that freedom and capitalism involve choices and casualties. Today the argument is about the community's obligations to its members who are hurt by capitalism's dynamism. In this argument the Democratic party, the world's oldest party, has a special responsibility. Just as the party must acquire foreign policies that acknowledge that the world is dangerous and there is little the United States can do to make it less so, the party also must acquire domestic policies that accept the fact that life is a corduroy road and there are limits to what government can or should do to smooth it.

# CONCLUSION

Even the weariest river runs somewhere to the sea and no matter how early a presidential campaign begins, it has a fixed destination—the first Tuesday after the first Monday in November of a year divisible by four. Some campaigns are like the Colorado River. Near the source they are cool and clear and strong and plentiful. Downstream they become silty and disappear into the sand. But most campaigns are the reverse of that. They start muddy and become clarified, and clarifying. In the crucible of competition, the candidates learn their own minds and the public's mind. And both minds are shaped as well as discovered in the process. A wit once defined a barometer as an ingenious instrument that reveals the kind of weather we are experiencing. A presidential campaign is like that. It is a political barometer. But it does more than measure. It can change the climate.

As the curtain rises on any presidential nomination scramble, the electorate is generally in the "Is anyone *else* up there?" mood. The mood is explained by the following story.

A man walking along a cliff feels the ground crumble beneath his feet. He manages to clutch at a root extending from the face of the cliff, which saves him from falling to certain death on the jagged rocks amidst the crashing surf far below. But he cannot climb back to safety so he shouts up: "Is anyone up there?" A voice—the voice of God—fills the sky: "Have faith and pray. If you have sufficient faith and pray properly, you may let go and you will fall lightly as a feather, landing unhurt amidst the rocks and surf." The man looks back down at the rocks and surf, ponders the offer, and then shouts up: "Is anyone *else* up there?"

When the winnowing is over and two candidates are chosen, the mood of much of the electorate resembles that of Talleyrand who, when asked about Robespierre and Voltaire, said, "When I think of one, I prefer the other."

If recent history is a source of reliable inferences—and it is —two things may be confidently predicted. Both nominations will be settled before the conventions convene. And most voters will have made up their minds by the time the last leg of the marathon begins, around Labor Day.

Kefauver's upset of Adlai Stevenson in the 1956 New Hampshire primary invested primaries with new importance. Then Stevenson decided to express no preference regarding a running mate. Instead he allowed the convention to make the decision, and when Kefauver beat John Kennedy on the basis of proven strength in the primaries, Kennedy took note. Since then all conventions have been ratifying, not deciding, bodies. There has not been a second ballot for anything since 1956, when Stevenson set off that vice presidential scramble. And the decisions that conventions ratify are coming earlier and earlier in the political season. In 1968 only 1 percent of the delegates were chosen by March 15. In 1988 54 percent will be chosen by March 15.

In a *Los Angeles Times* exit poll in November, 1984, 47 percent of the respondents said they had decided before the first primary in February who they would vote for in November, and another 21 percent had decided before September. Of course in a year like 1984, when there is an ideologically well-defined incumbent challenged by an equally well-defined rival who, like the incumbent, has been on the national stage for two decades, the undecided vote is apt to be especially small. But in almost every election, the post-convention contest is for the support of a moveable minority.

It is less clear whether the election will be close. Only ten elections since 1789 have been close, meaning won by a margin of approximately 3 percent or less. But close elections seem to come in clusters. Five were consecutive (1876–1892) and three were recent (1960, 1968, 1976).

The 1988 presidential race will resemble the mule race that Mark Twain said had an absence of harmony that was well compensated for by conspicuous variety. The variety will not include political extremes. Leave aside Jesse Jackson. He is not running for President; he is using the process for other political purposes. Among the other candidates none will be to the left of the fish fork or to the right of the soup spoon. It is important to understand that in American politics the success and fun is in middlingness.

In Peter De Vries's novel about the sexual revolution arriving in Iowa, the protagonist is invited to an orgy, where he quickly acquires the nickname "Vanilla." The nickname is a disparaging comment on his adherence to the sexually mundane in spite of the 27 other flavors available.[1] In presidential politics, as in other orgies, a vanilla person will get bad reviews from the critics. But non-vanilla politics need not be immoderate. What vanilla means in politics is un-fun.

It is arguable that the most volatility-inducing ingredient in the life of the developed bourgeois world is not any political ideology or religious passion. Rather, it is boredom. Boredom accounts for many cultural and literary fads. It accounts for much, perhaps most, abuse of drugs for recreational purposes. It has been said that most modern entertainments, from television to heroin, are methods of obliterating consciousness. It sometimes seems that the state of consciousness most prevalent and most onerous, at least among materially comfortable populations, is boredom. We are prodigiously frantic at inventing pastimes. An interesting word, that: "pastime." Baseball is "the national pastime." We seek diversions "to help us pass the time." It is a peculiar idea; time will pass with no help from any of us. And it is unlikely that a fourteenth century peasant tilling the fields—someone else's fields—from sunup to sundown ever fretted about the difficulty of whiling away the idle hours with a pastime. Idle hours are a modern luxury.

Robert Nisbet writes that boredom, although not a quantifiable variable in history comparable to war, disease, famine, economic depression, is nevertheless among the most insistent and universal forces that have shaped human behavior. Man is apparently uniquely capable of boredom. Cows look bored. Hamsters on treadmills ought to be bored, if they have any sense. A clam's life lacks zip. But, says Nisbet, probably only a nervous system as developed as man's is capable of boredom.[2]

According to one theory, that nervous system evolved over millions of years during which man (and perhaps his immediate predecessor) lived with saber-toothed tigers and hairy mammoths and other such exciting creatures lurking around every corner. Vigilance was called for in such a stimulating environment. Then suddenly, in a period of a few thousand years—a mere blink in the history of the species—saber-toothed tigers have been thin on the ground, much of the ground has become paved and policed and life has lost much of the sort of snap, crackle and pop that kept cave persons on their toes. It is to snap, crackle and pop that mankind's nervous system is, by evolution, attuned.

Boredom plays a part in presidential politics. For many of the relatively few activists who are disproportionately important in the nominating process, politics is a—that word again —pastime. It can also simultaneously be an exercise of public spiritedness, a passionate and idealistic undertaking. Nevertheless, political activism often is a pastime, an antidote to boredom. The activists in American politics are above the national average in income, accumulated wealth and leisure time. To say that they are, more often than not, in it for the fun of it is not to say they are frivolous. Far from it. One sometimes wishes some activists were more alive to the fun of it and could rescue themselves, and the rest of us, from terminal earnestness. Most people in politics do not *just* want to have fun, but they do want to have fun.

Compared to war or narcotics, getting a crush on a candidate is a benign way to assuage boredom. But embracing a candidate is like ordering the blue-plate special. You get the whole thing. You really want the meat loaf and are content to swallow the mashed potatoes and slaw, but there usually is also something yucky thrown in, like lima beans. When evaluating candidates it is useful to try to divine their lima bean factor. If it is large, it spoils the fun.

The fact that political boys and girls want to have fun carries consequences, particularly in a situation as fluid as the 1988 race will be. A candidate who wants to energize activists had better be fun for the activists. Fun in America often is associated with novelty, so a candidate who has been around and conspicuous for many a moon may have difficulty crossing the fun threshold.

Ideas are fun. By ideas I do not mean a pastel endorsement of this or that particular technicality ("I proposed the amendment to the conference report on the Section 301c extension"). By ideas I mean primary colors nailed firmly to a tall mast. I mean a sense of what America is about and where it should be going. It is more fun to hear such ideas discussed than to hear a resume read.

A candidate is apt to have an advantage in terms of the entertainment quotient if he or she is not quite like the President he or she seeks to succeed. This is especially so if that President has been around for eight years. This advantage is apt to be especially important for candidates in the party of that President. The best thing for raising a politician's entertainment quotient is something anyone can have: ideas.

By 1984 Walter Mondale had been around the track in national politics many times. There was no inherent novelty. So with what idea did he try to compensate for the fact that his was an awfully familiar face? When he announced his candidacy in a chamber of the Minnesota state legislature he said, "I am ready." He said he was "ready" to be President. It would be hard to imagine a limper boast. Ready for what? Mondale then managed to get his campaign identified with an idea, all right, but it was old and not alluring. It was the idea that taxes should be raised. Mondale was right but managed to make the least of that asset. It was an old idea not redeemed by association with new visions.

Now, having said that candidates must act on the assumption that politics should not be boring, it must also be said that to avoid being boring it is not necessary to be passionate. But the pursuit of moderate goals can be a passionate undertaking.

Aside from the Revolutionary and Civil War eras, there have been four passionate periods in American politics. In the Jacksonian era the country was divided between two interests with fundamentally different visions of America, agrarian and commercial. In the turn-of-the-century "progressive" era there was a sense of social imbalance because of concentrated powers in political machines and industrial trusts. In the Depression there was a desire to expand the ameliorative function of the federal government, and that government's responsibility for economic management. In the 1960s and early 1970s there was corrosive skepticism about the competence and motives of government, an aroma of illegitimacy arising from perceived injustice (legally sanctioned segregation), incompetence (Vietnam) and scandal (Watergate). The heart of government, the presidency, was weakened by measures such as the War Powers Act and restrictions on impoundment. (The former limits the traditional presidential discretion in the use of military assets; the latter limits the freedom of the President to defer spending appropriated funds.)

Professor Samuel Huntington of Harvard says that this period of protest and exposure began February 1, 1960, when four black students conducted a sit-in at a segregated lunch counter in Greensboro, North Carolina. The period wanes in the mid-1970s, after the fall of Nixon and Saigon. The waning was welcome. It has been well said that, in a healthy democracy, politics takes place between the forty-yard lines. There should be only slight volatility, few rapid, wide swings of opinion. Scammon and Wattenberg offered this definition of American politics: An elephant and a donkey struggling to place all eight legs on a dime placed exactly on the fifty-yard line, equidistant from each sideline.[3] The secret of American politics generally is to be, or at least to be seen to be, middling: in the middle of the road, and in the middle of the general range of human virtues and aspirations. And it does not hurt to come from the middle of the country, which Ohio can claim to be, symbolically if not geographically. Since Ohio came into the Union (1803), there have been only nine occasions when a candidate won the White House without winning Ohio. In this century, only two Presidents (FDR, in 1944, and JFK) have done so.

Aside from moderation, almost all successful candidates, especially in the modern age, have one thing in common. They are unusual in the way referred to in Broder's Law. That law (named after its author, columnist David Broder, the Newton of the physics of politics) is that anyone who desires to run for President, especially now that there seem to be more state primaries than there are states, reveals by his desire to run that he is too loony to be trusted with the office. Broder's premise is that the desire to run for President may be public-spirited but certainly is peculiar. However, some undertakings are so grindingly arduous that they cannot be done well except by persons who relish the draining strain. Being a surgeon is one; being a professional lineman is another; being a presidential candidate is a third.

Why do they do it? For the same reason people do lots of things—for lots of reasons. Freud noted that there are artists who give up the pursuit of fame, wealth and love of beautiful women to devote their energies to their art, in the hope that their art will bring them fame, wealth and the love of beautiful women. Presidential candidates are not frivolous people. They want power. They want power to do things. They want to do things because they think the things ought to be done. And the language of "oughts" is the language of moral duty.

To understand what makes many candidates run it helps to understand what makes life in the legislative branch so frustrating to people with the healthy political desire to run things. Running things is an essentially executive satisfaction.

Since the invention of broadcasting, the presidency has become especially prominent, and people tend to equate prominence with power. But most of the time under most Presidents prior to FDR there was congressional ascendancy. The system of checks and balances has generally been tilted toward the legislative branch.

The argument for presidential ascendancy is that the President is the only officer of government capable of eliciting a national mandate or advancing national strategies for domestic and international affairs. On the other hand, perhaps it is fortunate that, under current allocations of power, presidential ascendancy requires a rare combination of political circumstances and personal capacities. Considering the run of Presidents, it is arguable that there is generally more wisdom in Congress, collectively, than in the individual in the Oval Office.

Before Woodrow Wilson was a politician he was a political scientist. (That was before students of government fancied themselves scientists.) In that capacity he wrote a book about the federal government. The book was titled *Congressional Government*. He wrote it before he had even seen Congress or one of its committees. He was disturbed by the domination, as he saw it, of the government by the legislative branch. Wilson never served in a legislature. He was first President of Princeton University, then chief executive of New Jersey, then chief executive of the United States. He was one of the men who, by his vision and energy, enlarged the office of the presidency and put the nation on the path to presidential government. As a result, the political geography of Washington is now sixteen blocks askew.

Jenkin's Hill, now Capitol Hill, is where the quadrants of the District of Columbia touch. Geography serves political symbolism: Congress is, in theory, central. But by its own actions—paradoxically, by its energy in mandating energetic government—Congress has pushed itself to the periphery. The federal machinery can, indeed generally must, run without the close supervision of the mechanic that put it together.

As the presidency has become the symbolic and energizing center of the federal government, Congress has become a source of presidential candidates eager for the special satisfactions of executive experience. In 1988 at least two members of the House of Representatives are going to try to take the giant step from that chamber to the Oval Office. Jack Kemp (R., N.Y.) and Richard Gephardt (D., Mo.) have a lot of history against them. The House is not known as the Mother of Presidents. Only James Garfield went directly from the House to the White House. However, in 1976 Rep. Morris Udall (D., Ariz.) lost four primaries (New Hampshire, Massachusetts, Wisconsin, Michigan) to Jimmy Carter by fewer votes than Oklahoma's Senator Fred Harris (quit pretending, you don't remember him) siphoned off from Udall's liberal base. Had Udall won even two of those primaries, he would have been nominated.

The Senate, on the other hand, has in recent years become a hatchery of candidates. It is said that there is a statue in every stone, and a presidential candidate in every Senator. One reason Senators want to rise is that being a Senator is less fun than it used to be, in part because of policies favored by liberals. The number of federal programs has grown geometrically while the number of Senators and Congressmen, 535, has grown not at all. So they lead lives of mounting frustration and diminishing reflection. Their time is fractioned to the point of madness, with less and less time devoted to legislating and more and more time devoted to serving as ombudsmen mediating conflicts between the central government and local governments that seem unable to fix the firehouse roof without some federal involvement.

Before Howard Baker put down his mace of office (no, he did not really have one, which is a pity) as Majority Leader in order to prepare—or so he thought—for a run for the White House, he had a thought. It was both piquant and poignant, and as anachronistic as an Amish buggy. He proposed that Senators be paid just $36,000, in seven monthly installments, January through July. If the Senate loiters longer, let Senators receive only a small per diem. This proposal, sincerely made, came from a good but exasperated Senator throwing up his hands and throwing in the towel. Baker has long said that no one should be a professional legislator. Legislators should be farmers, merchants, teachers, lawyers. The citizen-legislator should be a legislator secondarily and temporarily. But Baker was affirming Jeffersonian values in a Hamiltonian setting, in an industrialized society administered by a strong central government. Baker had grown bone-weary leading a Congress that is attempting to hold too many reins in its hands. Under Baker's proposal, Congress would assemble to express sentiments and then would depart, melancholy perhaps, but reconciled to the reality of executive ascendancy in the modern state.

Americans seem to invoke Jeffersonian values—decentralization, local control, small and amateur government—more insistently as those values become more obviously irrecoverable. In 1980 Americans even decided to put an ardent Jeffersonian—Ronald Reagan—at the center of a government more mighty than anything Hamilton ever imagined. The controlling fact is this: Fifty years ago there were 435 Congressmen and 96 Senators. Today there are 435 Congressmen and 100 Senators. The number of legislators is fixed; the legislature's work load has grown exponentially. So the legislature's work is increasingly done elsewhere, no matter what you read in your high school civics text. The work is done in bureaucracies that write the regulations that effectively turn vague legislative expressions of goals into laws. And the work that is done by the legislature is increasingly done by legislative staffs.

The growth of congressional staff also reflects a primal urge in institutions. Professor James Q. Wilson of UCLA argues that organizations come to resemble the organizations with which they are in constant conflict. Senator Moynihan has elaborated this insight into the Iron Law of Emulation.[4] He notes that Teddy Roosevelt in 1902 built the West Wing of the White House, where the Oval Office is. Until then, Presidents and their staffs of three or four worked in the President's living room. In 1903 the House voted itself its first office building. In 1904 the Senate did likewise. "Originally," Moynihan says, "a senator's office was his desk on the Senate floor. These desks proved inadequate, and in the 1830s three-inch-high mahogany writing boxes were added to the desks. Daniel Webster refused to have his desk altered on the grounds that if his predecessor could have done without the additional space, so could he."[5] By 1978, Moynihan says, the Senate alone had a budget larger than the budget of seventy-four countries.

But bigger is certainly not more fun. The elephantiasis of Congress has been accompanied by a decline in job satisfaction on the part of the 535 people who work there because they won elections. A sense of having slight control over their time and energies is one reason why Congressmen and Senators seek the presidency, and why Governors, having had the satisfaction of executive office, try to become the biggest executive of all.

So much for why they do it. Now on to the question of how they do it.

In American politics the science is simple. There are two variables—numbers and intensity. You need a cadre of intense supports to help win the required gross number of voters. So much for the science. The complexity of American politics is in the artistry—the execution.

The late Fred Astaire, a severe perfectionist, once said to a dance partner, "Don't be nervous—but don't make any mistakes." You can imagine how helpful that was. That is the beginning, and very nearly the end, of useful rules for candidates. But if you insist on science, begin by accepting the fact that politics, like medicine, is a peculiar science. In medicine there are myriad experts, specializations, data, jargon and technologies. But the explanation of a medical event often involves some hoary maxim such as, "Eat and exercise sensibly."

There are three publics that matter in the nomination scramble and the general election. There is the political and journalistic menagerie inside the Washington beltway; there are the party activists; and then there are gobs of other people (a.k.a. America). Although the first and second groups sometimes are reluctant to admit it, the third group is in control. And that group's likes and dislikes are not mysterious or irrational.

In January, 1977, with Republican fortunes at a low ebb, Bill Brock (former Congressman and Senator from Tennessee; later, Secretary of Labor, among other things, in the Reagan administration) became party chairman and said: There is nothing wrong with the party that 12 percent inflation won't cure. The October, 1980, inflation rate? Twelve percent. Raging inflation debases the currency, discourages the virtue of thrift and rewards unproductive speculation. Inflation is the sort of concern that jolly well ought to influence votes. It cannot be said too often: Voters are not fools. That must be said often because of our national penchant for explaining elections in trivializing terms.

Many—perhaps millions—who watched Ronald Reagan shinny up to the top of the greasy pole of American politics remain convinced that he did it all on a smile and a shoeshine, and that the shoeshine was not really important. This explanation has a problem or two.

Reagan won, then won again, and got a significant portion of his way in Washington. If all that happened because of his smile, his shrug, his nod, his breathy, "Well, . . ." then why did he not win the Republican nomination he first wanted, in 1968? Why did he lose the 1976 nomination to Ford? Back then he had the same smile, shrug, nod and "Well, . . ."

The obsession with Reagan's "salesmanship" on the campaign trail became an obsession with his prowess as the "Great Communicator" in power. This preoccupation became intense after his successful televised appeal to the country on behalf of his economic program in the summer of 1981. But Reagan's tax victory should not have been taken as another sign that the Great Communicator was irresistible. The success of his televised appeals to the country was related to what he was asking the country to do. The Great Communicator was asking it to be brave and endure a tax cut. Heck, if you stand on my stoop and shout, "Let's go get pizza!" you'll get a stunning response from neighborhood children. But that doesn't make you a great communicator.

Many Democratic professionals never came close to understanding the extent to which the Reagan product has always been inextricably bound up with the salesman's persona. As William A. Henry wrote in his book on the 1984 campaign, Reagan occasionally attained "the ultimate goal of every national politician: to embody so thoroughly the myths and traits of the country's idealized image of itself that a vote for Ronald Reagan would be a vote for the real America."[6] Such embodiment is not salesmanship, or at least not merely sales-manship. It is a political product. It is a kind of leadership and is consequential.

Democrats, convinced that Reagan's successes were con-sequences of cosmetics, decided in 1984 that their task was to "separate the salesman from the product." They wanted to say to the voters: "Yes, yes, of course, he *is* charming. Splen-did fellow. Love to sit next to him at dinner. Were he fifty years younger you would want him to marry your daughter. But you really do not favor his policies, and their effects will linger long after the smile has faded." The Democrats were overestimating the powers of salesmanship.

Scammon and Wattenberg noted that the politics of the post-war era have been fertile with trivializing explanations of presidential elections. In 1948, we have been told, Truman won because Dewey looked like the little man on the wed-ding cake.[7] Eisenhower won in 1952 and 1956 because he reminded us of our fathers. Kennedy won because Nixon used lousy make-up and the wrong color suit in the first de-bate. Johnson won in 1964 because Goldwater won the Re-publican nomination because the second Mrs. Rockefeller gave birth on the eve of the winner-take-all California pri-mary. Nixon won in 1968 because Mayor Daley's police were naughty during the Democratic convention in Chicago. Nixon won in 1972 because McGovern was a terrible candidate nominated because Edmund Muskie wept during the New Hampshire primary. Carter won in 1976 because Ford, in the second debate, said that Poland is free from Soviet domina-tion. Reagan won the 1980 nomination by saying, in Nashua, New Hampshire, "I paid for this microphone," and he won the election because, in the debate with Carter, he said "There you go again." Reagan won in 1984 because he was "good at" television and Mondale was not. And so it goes.

This sort of explanation of political events seems to be a product of the post-war era, perhaps for several reasons. Par-adoxically, this penchant for simple, not to say simpleminded, explanations may be a result of the new sophistication and complexity of campaigning. As the machinery of politics—polling, direct mail, and all the rest—has become more elaborate, there have been more nuts and bolts for political journalists to know about. Political journalism has become more preoccupied with mechanisms and cosmetics. Television, especially, has encouraged the notion that a vivid gesture or memorable "sound bite" seen by millions of people at a dramatic juncture of a campaign must be as consequential as it is conspicuous.

Theodore White had a reporter's tendency to believe that vivid events are as important as they are vivid. He wrote, wrongly, that Ronald Reagan won the 1980 New Hampshire primary by seizing the microphone at the Nashua debate. Actually, Reagan had surged ahead well before that. Perhaps journalistic narcissism makes journalists think that communications technologies are the levers that move history—hence White's obsession with television. He called it "the most unsettling event in Western Society since the invention of printing."[8] However it is easy to make too much—and White did —of the Republican delegate in 1968 who said he could not switch from Nixon to Reagan because, "I told CBS that I'm voting for Nixon. I'm pledged to CBS."[9]

O! Television! It is the obsession of the era. It is time to say something about what it does, and what it does not do.

It has been said that once when Disraeli was canvassing for votes door to door, a woman opened the door and Disraeli paused, then, explaining his pause, exclaimed: "I was overcome by the resemblance to my sainted mother—and she was a very beautiful woman." Candidates no longer win by canvassing door to door, dispensing charm like Disraeli. (His gallantry was all the more gallant because it was politically wasted: the woman could not vote.) They stomp into our living rooms via television. They get on television because they are newsworthy, and because they are products that pay to advertise themselves.

Suppose in the campaign's final sixty days each candidate averages two minutes on the evening news. In that case the period after Labor Day is the final 240 minutes of the campaign. True, there also are paid media, but their job is to amplify themes established on the evening newscasts. However, paid media mesmerize political journalists and reformers.

There is in Washington a monument to the reformers of the 1970s. It is a bureaucracy—the Federal Election Commission —that enforces congressionally imposed limits on the permissible quantity of political speech. Money is indispensable for political communication. To say you are for unabridged freedom of speech and for strict spending limits is like saying you are for an unabridged right to read and for strict rationing of paper. Reformers in the 1970s severely limited the amounts that individuals or groups can give to a candidate. So candidates must spend less time talking about issues and more time hustling money in smaller dollops. The limits on giving encourage candidates to accept federal financing, which entails spending limits. So in nomination contests candidates are allowed to spend $24 million, less than Frito-Lay spends to promote a thicker potato chip.

It is arguable that advertising of all sorts is too much with us. But it has been that way for many a moon. Flying over Nebraska in the summer of 1943, an Englishman was struck by the "normality—hundreds of miles of it and not a sight or sound to remind one that this was a country at war." Then his lunch tray arrived, and inscribed on the pat of butter was an injunction: "REMEMBER PEARL HARBOR." Of course they knew there was a war on. However, Americans believe that a bit of advertising never hurts. The question of political importance is: How much advertising helps a lot?

One of the most impressive barrages of political advertising on television was Nixon's in October, 1968. The barrage was, at that point, much the most expensive in history. And it coincided with a dramatic and almost decisive swing of votes toward Hubert Humphrey. Gallup estimated that about 200,000 votes per day were moving to Humphrey that month.

Advertising is not always effective, but it is central to the ethos and functioning of our commercial republic. In Arthur Miller's play *The Price* a character says: "Years ago a person, he was unhappy, didn't know what to do with himself—he'd go to church, start a revolution—*something*. Today you're unhappy? Can't figure it out? What is the salvation? Go shopping." [10] Verily, go shopping for pantyhose or Presidents. But the fact of advertising does not make shopping an activity driven by irrationality. Advertising is a complex and somewhat paradoxical phenomenon.

Advertising promises a flowering of individuality as persons define themselves in choices. Yet advertising presupposes mass tastes. Advertising promises a democratic distribution of pleasure, but sells many goods by stressing exclusivity—the idea that the purchaser will elevate himself above the herd. Advertising celebrates choice—"consumer sovereignty"—yet stirs anxieties about whether human volition is sovereign over manufactured persuasion. Advertising performs an (often minimal) informing function necessary for rational choice. But advertising assumes that consumers often are impulsive and suggestible. The average supermarket stocks about 10,000 different brands and products. If each customer bought only what he came to the store intending to buy, supermarkets would be very different. They depend on impulse buying. Some impulses are triggered by previous exposures to advertising.

One hundred years ago, Americans read advertisements just to ascertain the availability of goods to satisfy elemental needs—food, clothes, tools. Now they read advertisements to ascertain what they might decide they desire. Certain necessities (soap, toothpaste) are heavily advertised, but it sometimes seems that half the GNP is generated by personal anxieties—about bad breath, damp underarms.

Those gorgeous "Miller time" commercials make no claim.

They create a mood and are weapons in a market-share battle. They do not try to get you to buy a Miller beer rather than a Buick, or to make you thirsty, or to get you to buy Miller rather than Dr. Pepper when you are thirsty. They aim to get beer drinkers to drink Miller rather than some other beer.

Advertising is less a science of persuasion than an art of arresting attention briefly so that perhaps some commercially useful response will occur, sometime. Arresting attention is increasingly difficult as Americans become inured to sensory blitzkriegs. Life in America makes Americans into good auditors of advertising. They develop a sort of filter in their inner ears which catches much advertising as if it were audible lint. Much advertising is, in effect, audible wallpaper. It is there, all around us, but is not noticed.

In politics especially, there comes a point at which the dollars spent have sharply declining utility. Republicans learned that in the dismal (for Republicans) experience of the 1986 Senate elections. In the thirty-four races, Republican candidates spent $122 million, $33 million more than did Democratic candidates ($89 million). Republican candidates outspent Democratic candidates in twenty-three of the thirty-four races. But Democrats won twenty of the thirty-four. In the thirteen closest races, those decided by 6 percentage points or less, Democrats won ten and Republicans won three. Of those, Republican candidates outspent Democratic candidates in eleven out of thirteen.

The guy in Idaho was joking when he said it would have been less expensive in 1986 if, instead of strafing the state with television commercials, the two Senate candidates had just taken the undecided voters out to dinner. But the guy was right. About 70 percent of Idaho's 515,000 registered voters were expected to vote that Tuesday. Since Labor Day only about 7 percent of those likely voters had been undecided. The two candidates threw more than $5 million at the 25,000 undecideds, or $200 per voter. That would buy a feast in Boise.

By election day Idaho knew how veal scaloppine feel. Many states were pounded flat by the merciless attentions of people seeking admission to the Senate. The pounding hammers were negative television commercials that rarely rose to the level of lowbrow.

The most expensive 1986 race was California's. The two Senate candidates spent $20 million. But on a per capita basis, that was a bargain-basement campaign. California's race involved $1.55 for each of the 12.8 million registered voters. Next door in Nevada the $3.5 million race involved about $10 for each of the 356,384 registered voters.

What money made possible in 1986 was a mass conversion of candidates to the Dick Butkus Doctrine of Political Manners. Butkus, a maiming linebacker for the Chicago Bears, once said, "I wouldn't ever set out to hurt anybody deliberately unless it was, you know, important—like a league game or something." In 1986 "going negative"—doing unto your opponent before he could do unto you—was the preferred style.

There are always excuses for going too far in any contest. When Sugar Ray Robinson landed a punch after the bell had ended a round, the ringside broadcaster explained, "It's hard to hear the bell up there. There's a tremendous amount of smoke here in the Boston Garden." In 1986 three excuses were offered for negative campaigning. "The other guy started it." And "I'm not being negative, I'm just alerting the electorate to my loathsome opponent's squalid record." And "Negative campaigning is as American as apple pie—and, by the way, did I mention that my opponent hates apple pie."

True, American politics has always had a bare-knuckle side. "Ma, Ma, where's my Pa?" was a Republican reference to Democrat Grover Cleveland's illegitimate child. Democrats added the defiant line, "Gone to the White House, ha, ha, ha." Cleveland's 1884 opponent was James G. Blaine. "Blaine, Blaine, James G. Blaine, continental liar from the state of Maine." Somewhat negative, that. But television has unique immediacy. Today voters do not venture out to experience negativism at torchlight rallies. Today negativism comes to voters in their living rooms.

In 1986 Congressman Bob Edgar was criticized for negative ads he used against Pennsylvania's Republican Senator, Arlen Specter. Edgar's response was that the 1986 campaigns were not much, if any, more negative than many campaigns have been. The difference, he said, is that the gusher of political money has made the negativism more audible. That is, candidates have always said beastly things about one another in speeches at union halls or lodge meetings, but now that there is so much cash sloshing around in the system, candidates can afford to broadcast their attacks.

There is a lot of money around, and it goes a long way in some states. Horace Busby notes that four of the fiercest contests in 1986 were for Republican-held seats in four of the least populous states: Idaho, Nevada, South Dakota and North Dakota, ranked forty-first, forty-third, forty-fifth and forty-sixth respectively. They have a combined population of 2.7 million, about half the population of Cook County, Illinois. Television time is cheap out where the deer and the antelope outnumber the voters. In Dakota Territory you can buy thirty seconds of time on "The Cosby Show" for just $800.

What is new is not just the amount of negativism, it is the niggling tendentiousness of it. Only a candidate sitting on a large and solid lead feels he can be too principled to run negative ads. (New York's Republican Senator Al D'Amato was always so far ahead in 1986 he felt no need for negative ads. Too bad. His campaign manager's name was Rick Nasti.) And there is nothing wrong with criticizing the public record of public people. What is tiresome is the reckless use of a candidate's votes to characterize the candidate. A vote for less-than-maximum funding for a program for the handicapped or against the most stringent sanctions against South Africa becomes grounds for thirty-seconds of rubbish about

the candidate "voting against the handicapped" or "supporting apartheid."

One reason for the recourse to negative ads is that in recent
years they have worked. Another reason is that in 1986 the
issues were so unsatisfying. The top ten issues were: drugs,
drugs, drugs, drugs, drugs, drugs, drugs, drugs, drugs and the
deficit. Drugs is the conservatives' money-throwing issue:
"Don't just stand there, Hoss, throw some money at the problem!" But after Congress has denounced drugs and the deficit, and has made the latter worse by throwing money at the
former, the situation remains as follows. No one really knows
what the federal government can do effectively against drugs.
Everyone knows what it can do about the deficit (cut spending or increase taxes, or both) and no one wants to do
anything.

So grown men with too much money, too few ideas and too
little respect for the voters get into slanging matches, such as
the one in South Dakota in 1986. There the Republican incumbent Senator accused his opponent of accepting a contribution from Jane Fonda. And that sin was made scarlet by the
fact—so said the Senator—that Fonda hates a South Dakota
export, red meat. However, the Democrat did not personally
get a contribution from Fonda. She attended a fund-raiser for
all Democratic Senate candidates. And South Dakotans were
assured that on a recent trip she pulled into a McDonald's
and devoured two Big Macs. It seems somehow right that
the 1986 political season ended with a Senate contest
and perhaps the fate of the free world hinged on voters'
reactions to the news that Jane Fonda suffered a Big Mac
attack.

Negative advertising sometimes succeeds, in part because
people tend to confuse rudeness with sincerity and to equate
sincerity with high principle. However, if negative advertising worked most of the time, then most of the time we would
be governed by the richest and nastiest. We are not. The
electorate is not a debased, manipulated mob. They are seri-

ous about what is serious in politics. The serious stuff is not advertising and is not any other nut or bolt.

America has a surplus of people who know everything about the nuts and bolts of politics. They can name all the county chairmen in Indiana and tell you the cost of thirty seconds of drive-time radio in Denver. But they do not have a clue as to why Americans pull one voting lever rather than another. So let us say something for a reason Saul Bellow gave in *Mr. Sammler's Planet:* ". . . it is sometimes necessary to repeat what all know. All mapmakers should place the Mississippi in the same location, and avoid originality. It may be boring, but one has to know where he is. We cannot have the Mississippi flowing toward the Rockies for a change."[11] So let's just blurt out this truth: Americans vote for candidates they think they agree with.

In 1980, to the despair of many advisers and creative advertisers, Reagan insisted on relying heavily on "talking head" ads. There were no fancy production values. But it turned out the candidate knew something. Americans want to hear what is in a candidate's head. In 1984 Reagan could rely on gooey "feel good" ads filmed in orange sunsets because by then people knew what was in his head. Even so, he paid the price for the vacuousness of the 1984 campaign. Even before the Iran-contra affair blew his administration's transmission, his second term had been sputtering along on too few cylinders. The 1984 landslide was shaped by a campaign too themeless to impart the momentum that comes from a practical, specific mandate.

Here is a fact that should be printed on both parties' brains with letters of brass: The candidate who has received more votes for President than anyone in American history is that telegenic charmer Richard Nixon. He got the votes because —I apologize for the banality—lots of voters liked what he said, and took what he said more seriously than his manner of saying it. The best politicians understand that voters are like that.

The real concerns of voters are not cosmetic matters, but neither are they constants. Saturation journalism, especially on television, quickly wears out most issues, or at least the public's interest in them. For example, after the 1984 conventions there was a two-week flurry of reporting, punditry and full-court-press panel-show-itis on the subject of the interaction of religious and political activism. The people who were alarmed by the role of clergy in politics on behalf of Reagan were people who had been, to say no more, unperturbed by the political roles previously played by the Reverend Martin Luther King and the Reverend William Sloane Coffin and others. They were not noticeably perturbed by the role played in 1984 by the Reverend Jesse Jackson, who campaigned more from pulpits than from any other place. But suddenly in the late summer of 1984 the talkative class was seized with anxiety about "the religious right." Fortunately, it took only about two weeks for saturation journalism to pound into a shapeless pulp the Good-Lord-(If-You-Will-Pardon-the-Expression)-Religion-and-Politics-Are-Getting-Tangled-Up-in-this-Nation-Begun-by-Pilgrims issue.

Yeats heard an old man say, sadly, "All that's beautiful drifts away like the water." If you listen carefully you will hear wise politicians say, contentedly, that in American politics almost everything in the way of issues, beautiful or not, passes away like the controversy about fluoridated water. Remember when the policy of putting fluoride in drinking water was a political issue? How about the John Birch Society, that small unmerry band that journalists contrived to present as a menace to the Republic in 1964?

Try to tell a teenager today that thirty years ago the nation was riven over the question of whether blacks could eat at lunch counters. The teenager will look at you as though you are telling anthropological tales from a lost continent. In a sense, you are.

In 1960 John Kennedy had to deal with deep-seated resistance to the idea of a Catholic President, a cultural attitude that now seems as prehistoric as, say, the practice of requiring people with black skin to sit in the back of the bus. But a less-known fact from that time is an even more startling illustration of how changeable America is. After winning the election Kennedy repaired to Palm Beach to begin the selection of his Cabinet. There he offered the post of Attorney General to Connecticut's Governor (later Senator) Abraham Ribicoff. Ribicoff refused to accept it, arguing that the nation—especially the nation poised on the edge of civil rights turmoil— was not ready for a Jewish Attorney General.

A minority of the readers of this book can rewind the tapes of their memories back forty years. But if you can remember 1948 you remember that Alfred Kinsey, a midwestern revolutionary (he taught at Indiana University in Bloomington), published the first volume of his "Report." Writing with the cool immersion in detail appropriate to a professor of zoology, which he was, he showed that Americans were sexually . . . well, busy. He seems to have been startled that people were shocked by his statistician's tone of voice when he said things like: It is not surprising that some teenagers are sexually active, considering that there are 450,000 instances of fornication among residents of Indiana each week. But decorousness was in vogue at a time when *The New York Times* changed an advertisement for "naughty but nice" lingerie to "Paris-inspired—but so nice." And a nightclub advertisement of "50 of the hottest girls this side of hell" became "50 of the most alluring maidens this side of paradise." Four years later, *Playboy* came hopping along and decorum has not been the same.

Political passions often rise and fall as a result of provocations issuing from the changing culture, the changes of which are largely autonomous in the sense that they drive rather than are driven by political choices. In recent years cultural changes have aroused political passions that seek outlets in constitutional changes. In the first four months of 1981, more than 145 constitutional amendments were offered dealing with the budget, busing, school prayers, abortion, judges' tenure, making English the nation's official language, banning racial quotas and changing the amendment process. Fortunately, although more than 10,000 amendment proposals have been introduced in Congress since 1789, only 33 have been sent on to the states, and only 26 have become amendments.

There is a streak of anti-constitutional radicalism in contemporary conservatism. The 1980 Republican Platform speaks of selecting judges "who respect . . . the sanctity of innocent human life." But it would be wrong to seek (and hard to find) thoughtful judges who would hold that the Fourteenth Amendment protections of "persons" extend to fetuses. Any Justice who would purport to find authority for that in the Constitution would be just as arrogantly legislative, anti-judicial and result-oriented as were the Justices who, in 1973, overturned the abortion laws that reflected the community judgments of fifty states. Such a new Justice would be just as guilty as the 1973 Court was of an authoritarian shortcut around the democratic process, using litigation rather than legislation to impose social change.

The truly conservative criticism of the 1973 ruling is not simply that it was incoherent in its attempt to find a right to abortion in the Constitution (a right supposedly inhering in a recently discovered right to privacy). Rather, the basic conservative complaint is that the 1973 ruling used—abused—the Constitution as a pretext for nationalizing a question that traditional and correct construction of the Constitution had treated as a moral judgment to be settled by the political processes of the states.

By 1989 Reagan will have appointed 45 percent of all sitting federal judges. But conservatives will find Reagan's judges exasperatingly conservative. Sensitive to the organic growth of the law, they will not kick over the traces of precedents that have established liberal law on such matters as reverse discrimination, pornography, abortion.

Suppose the improbable: Suppose the Supreme Court produced a five-person majority for overturning the 1973 abortion decision. That would just ignite fifty state arguments about regulation of abortion. The court could restore the legal conditions of 1973, but the social conditions are vastly different, and conservatives, especially, should know that laws cannot fly in the face of attitudes. Today there are many more than 1 million abortions a year. It is the nation's second most common surgical procedure, after circumcision. For six summers the most popular President in a generation has supported the constitutional amendment to restore the status quo ante 1973. It did not even pass the Republican-controlled Senate in six years. Nor has the school-prayer amendment. The steam is seeping out of the social issues. (A peculiarity of our increasingly peculiar political vocabulary is that the phrase "social issues" is used to distinguish certain controversies from, of all things, economic issues. The latter concern who shall have how much food, shelter, clothing, security and fun, and it is odd to talk in a way that distinguishes such matters from social issues.) They will still energize intense constituencies, but decreasingly so because those voters will know, deep down, that no foreseeable election will achieve their goals.

That certainly is true regarding the original social issue, crime, particularly "crime in the streets," meaning mugging and other young men's crimes. In 1983, in one out of every five households, someone suffered an assault, burglary, larceny, rape or robbery. Few of the criminals involved were or will be caught, and fewer will be prosecuted, and fewer still will be convicted. In California, where one-tenth of the electorate lives (lives anxiously, evidently), a reliable poll reveals that crime is now the foremost concern. Yet crime was not an issue in the 1984 presidential campaign. One reason is that crime was declining. For the first time in twenty years the crime rate had declined in two consecutive years.

However, the main reason crime is not an issue is not that the crime rate has changed. It is that the electorate has changed. It recognizes that federal policy is peripheral to the problem. So it goes, as yesterday's hot issues are cooled by the winds of social change.

Those winds shape the nation's agenda. The simple question that the electorate puts to all presidential aspirants is, "What do you want to do?" But no winner ever gets to do quite what he wants. Candidates propose agendas, history disposes of them. John F. Kennedy did not plan on struggling with the House Rules Committee. Lyndon B. Johnson wanted to concentrate on building the second stage of the Roosevelt revolution, not on "nation-building" in Indochina. Gerald Ford, after a career in the minority in the less-glamorous half of the legislative branch, just wanted to work the levers of government; instead he became preoccupied by Reagan's political challenge from the right. Richard Nixon and Jimmy Carter wound up utterly preoccupied with aberrational events (Watergate, the hostage crisis).

Most modern Presidents have come to feel that events are in the saddle and riding the political system. As Michael Barone notes,

> Richard Nixon came to office in 1969 in a nation still determined to expand the role of goverment and generally inclined to liquidate the American commitment in Vietnam. Nixon, against all his personal inclinations, presided over a government that saw domestic spending increase and defense spending decrease, that saw the development of a youth culture, the legalization of abortion, and the effective legalization of marijuana. Ideas that were abroad in the land moved the nation much more than the administration did, and well before Watergate. Then the Carter Administration came to office, staffed by people determined to continue in the direction opinion seemed to be moving around 1970, only to see the tide of opinion change. Now people wanted less government and a more aggressive, truculent foreign policy.[12]

The fact that Presidents are not perfectly autonomous does not vitiate the importance and dignity of elections. This nation's premise is that history is made not by impersonal forces but individuals' choices. However, since 1933 the choices have been becoming complicated faster than journalism has been becoming capable of clarifying complexities. History here is the history of the minds of free persons. Therefore, the quality of the history we shall make in the next fifty years depends to an unprecedented, and perhaps dismaying, extent on the quality of journalism.

Journalism should give less attention to the "inside story" of political tactics and more attention to the inner lives of the people who seek the most public of vocations. Prominent politicians are subjected to unremitting scrutiny, so they polish their surfaces until they shine like fine enamel. This whets our desire for some incision in the surface through which we might glimpse an interesting interior, something softer and less brittle than enamel.

Presidential campaigns are marvelous undesigned devices for piercing those surfaces. I say "undesigned" because what we have today is like Topsy: the system just grow'd. Ted Kennedy recalls that when his brother won the 1960 nomination only two primaries mattered much. John Kennedy's staff spent about six weeks in Wisconsin and then moved on for a long stay in West Virginia. Today's nomination ordeal is harrowing but the effect is good. The pressures on the candidates replicate those of the office they seek.

Peter Hart insists, "It comes down to values. Whatever is inside a candidate comes out in the presidential campaign. There is no hiding it." What should we hope to see revealed? Not just tactical cleverness of the sort that political reporters dwell upon—although such cleverness is required for the success of any presidency. What we should be looking for is a certain good-humored gravity—a cheerful seriousness that recognizes the importance of ideas and the habit history has of dealing harshly with ideas formulated out of power.

Many politicians are slow to acquire ideas and slower still to retire ideas. They acquire ideas slowly not because they are fastidious but because they are uninterested; hence the ones they wind up with often are, like the last loaves of bread on the store shelf, stale. Politicians interested in ideas are sometimes expected to produce new ones promiscuously. But if journalists had pounced on Aristotle, demanding new ideas, he might have babbled incoherently about "mixed regimes" and might have sounded like a ninny. Political ideas are not like plums, to be plucked one by one from some mental orchard. Creative politics is a pattern of responses by a seasoned temperament of society's vast inertia and small margin for change. When politicians succumb to fascination with a plump, juicy, spanking-new idea it is apt to be simple, splashy and oversold.

A British historian, Lewis Namier, once wrote: "What matters most about political ideas is the underlying emotions, the music to which ideas are a mere libretto, often of very inferior quality." The music of Reaganism has been a mood, a style, a posture, an aura. I believe that the music and the libretto have, on balance, met the nation's material and emotional needs tolerably well in the 1980s. But *A Chorus Line* is the only show that runs forever. The final curtain is coming down on Reagan and the winner in 1988 will promise "another opening, another show."

Republicans can no longer seek to win control of the government by bashing government. They must find a new vocabulary of conservatism, one that comes to terms with the three great lessons of the Reagan years. The first lesson is that the country is not nearly as conservative as it says it is. It expects—no, it demands—an activist government acting as an integrative force against the centripetal forces of American life. Second, American conservatives are not nearly as conservative as they say they are. They have long since come to terms with the legitimacy of the public's desire for a government energetic on behalf of their comfort, security and opportunity. Third, the rhythm of American politics guarantees that the new music will be a counterpoint to Reagan—probably a respectful counterpoint, and not very new. The difference will be an easy conscience about coming to terms with the rule of the modern state. Reagan did, so any Republican can.

The Democratic presidential candidate must come to terms with two plain facts. The first is that Reagan's tax cuts and the Democratic party's reluctance to raise taxes have necessitated new approaches for liberalism. The essence of liberalism is government direction of resources to accomplish social change. So the first task is to find resources. The largest reservoirs of resources are in the business sector and state governments. Liberals at the federal level can try to mandate certain uses of resources. They can provide incentives for private-sector provision of social services (although the tradition of using the tax code to structure incentives runs counter to the new reverence for "simplicity" in the tax code). Liberals can accept the devolution of responsiblities to state levels, and can content themselves with encouraging action there. Such devolution and encouragement of private-sector provision of services is an accommodation of liberal ends to conservative preferences regarding procedures.

There is today an oscillation of bewilderment in many democracies. The Democratic party's resurgence fits the European pattern. From Stockholm to the Hague, from Paris to Athens to Madrid, the left has been given a crack at the disagreeable business of reconciling yesterday's political promises and today's economic and demographic facts. In increasingly complex societies, with increasingly cumbersome governments, policy cycles and electoral cycles are decreasingly synchronized. Furthermore, wise policies often require short-term pains for long-term gains. But after the pains begin and before the gains arrive, policies are scrambled by intervening elections.

In Europe, as in the United States, the central political

argument is about how to make the welfare state compatible with the rate of economic growth necessary to finance the welfare state. In the United States the public is not being brought face-to-face with its needs and appetites, of the bill that will come due down the road, if the costs are not paid responsibly. The political class has not been telling the public the truth. A wit with a flair for euphemism, and an unrealized vocation for contemporary politics, once defined a fib as an artistic molding of the unshapely clay of truth. The nation is being fibbed to by its leaders.

Today the nation's mind is ambivalent, unformed—soft wax ready to receive fresh imprints. Horace Busby notes that 20 percent of those who voted in November, 1986, did so in eight states (Alabama, Alaska, California, Florida, Idaho, Illinois, New York, Pennsylvania) that elected four Democratic and four Republican governors while in each case choosing a Senator of the other party. Another clue to the country's mood is this: Of the thirteen new Senators, nine have served in the House, one has served there and in a Cabinet office (Brock Adams, Washington Democrat), three others have been Governors (Democrats Sanford of North Carolina and Graham of Florida and Republican Bond of Missouri). The electorate is in no mood for amateur hour in Washington. It craves competence.

The craving comes none too soon. Both parties have been representing the national mood with maddening fidelity. They suffer the same disability. They cannot propose policies proportionate to means, or means commensurate with policies.

The Democratic party is committed to programs of distributive justice—enhanced equality of conditions—that it is not prepared to ask the country to pay for. It has made itself hostage to Soviet intransigence by making arms control the centerpiece of U.S.-Soviet relations. And having made the achievement of agreements the test of any administration's facility in foreign policy, it is constantly tempted by unilateralism. To tranquilize turbulent areas such as Central America, Democrats are committed to reliance on an exported New Deal—economic development and the sort of negotiations that pacified labor-management relations in the auto industry in the 1930s. They will not recognize that some disputes cannot be brokered, and some negotiations presuppose a prior use of force.

The Republican party also has now made arms control the centerpiece of policy and the central drain on executive energies, notwithstanding the fact that no one can cite a single example of a great power's security being guaranteed or even significantly enhanced by arms control agreements. And the Republican party compounds the problem by its improper handling of its proper concern for rearmament. It is committed to more rearmament than it is prepared to ask the country to pay for. Its instincts are for an active world role involving costs, human and material, that public opinion will not sustain. The Republican party, too, is fully committed to a complex, ambitious menu of welfare state benefits, but it is not committed to requiring the generation that enjoys the benefits to pay for them. And even where Republicans differ reasonably from Democrats, they diminish their moral advantage by intellectual irresponsibility. Republicans define justice in terms more of equality of opportunity than of result, yet seem uninterested in the complexities of equal opportunity and the government's indispensable role in guaranteeing it.

The implacable persistence of such issues does not mean that it is unimportant which party runs the government. But it does suggest that any administration may have more latitude in deciding what to do about its agenda than in setting its agenda. However, a presidential election is as much of an agenda-setting moment as we have. They are the moments when this diverse, distracted, hectic, preoccupied, inattentive nation of restless individualists clears its throat, draws a deep breath and, for a brief moment, becomes conscious of itself as a collective enterprise.

The presidential electoral-vote system, and the custom of allocating state electoral votes on a winner-take-all basis, creates an illusion of mandate more emphatic than most Presidents really receive. In the television age, this is an optical illusion: In 1980, when 47.6 percent of the voters voted for Carter or Anderson, the electronic maps at the three networks turned almost solidly the Republican color.

This exaggeration of the clarity of the nation's decision can give a President-elect some momentum for respect. And it can give the country the invigorating (if inaccurate) sense of having said something clearly. That sense and that momentum are highly perishable. But every little bit helps in the struggle to invest government with more coherence than the country's mind usually has.

It is said that we are worn down less by the mountain we must climb than by the grain of sand in our shoe. The many irritants of our individual lives and of our political life often loom larger than the mountain we are climbing together, as a people, as we make democracy work. Thus we lose sight of the fact that this sort of mountain-climbing is more exhilarating than exhausting. So I end with a thought that has recurred in this meditation on the saga of American self-government: Politics is not everything, but it is something. It is something good, and agreeable, and fun, and serious.

The emancipation of women and the democratization of higher education have gone far toward opening careers to talents. The oral contraceptive, the jet engine, the cathode-ray tube and the silicon chip have done more than any election has done to change American life. We have compressed time by accelerating social change; we have obliterated physical distance by air travel; we have annihilated imaginative distance by communications technologies that make every sight and sound accessible to everyone.

However, in doing so we have jeopardized a capacity that distinguishes us from oysters—the capacity for astonishment. It is a paradox—and a problem—that as we have become more prolific with wonders, we have felt less wonder, even about the miracle of democracy.

Miracles are rare, but an American miracle recurs quadrennially. Nineteen eighty-eight can be a year for exuberant rediscovery. We are losing sight of the fact that we have made the rare into the routine. The peaceful disposition of power at regular intervals, which has been occurring here for two centuries, remains a rarity in human experience, even in the late twentieth century.

Journalists say: "Irritants are our business." They say: "We do not report the planes that land safely." Fine. Let them say that. But this, too, must be said: Good news is news.

A philosopher once said, "People have more fun than anybody." Quite right, and Americans have more fun than any other people, in part because their politics—their collective conversation—is so astonishingly amicable and, all things considered, intelligent. America's political system—the day-to-day success of it, the mundane miraculousness of it—is the big news of the modern world and, I think, of human experience.

# NOTES

## INTRODUCTION

1. Michael Barone and Grant Ujifusa, *The Almanac of American Politics: 1984* (Washington, D.C.: National Journal, 1983), "The Politics of Cultural Variety," p. xiv.

2. Ibid., p. xi.

3. Stephen Hess, "Why Great Men Still Are Not Chosen President," *The Brookings Review*, Summer 1987, p. 36.

4. Richard Brookhiser, *The Outside Story: How Democrats and Republicans Re-elected Reagan* (Garden City, New York: Doubleday & Company, Inc., 1986), pp. 3–6.

5. Ibid., p. 5.

6. Ibid., p. 3.


## RONALD REAGAN

1. Jeffrey Hart, *When the Going Was Good! American Life in the Fifties* (New York: Crown Publishers, Inc., 1982), p. 67.

2. Lionel Trilling, *The Liberal Imagination: Essays on Literature and Society* (Garden City, N.Y.: Anchor Books/Doubleday & Company, Inc., 1950, 1978), Preface, p. i.

3. Theodore White, *The Making of the President: 1964* (New York: Atheneum Publishers, 1965), p. 220.

4. Ibid., p. 313–14.

5. James Q. Wilson, "Why Reagan Won and Stockman Lost," *Commentary,* August 1986, p. 17.

6. Ibid., p. 17.

7. Correlli Barnett, *Bonaparte* (New York: Hill and Wang, 1978), Chapter IV, p. 60.

8. Joseph Epstein, *The Middle of My Tether, Familiar Essays* (New York, London: W. W. Norton & Company, 1983) "The Crime of a Happy Childhood," p. 222.

9. Ibid.

10. William A. Henry III, *Visions of America: How We Saw the 1984 Election* (Boston/New York: The Atlantic Monthly Press, 1985), p. 17.

## REPUBLICANS

1. Richard Wirthlin, in an interview with the author.

2. William Schneider, *American Elections of 1980,* Austin Ranney, ed. (Washington, D.C.: American Enterprise Institute, 1981), Chapter 7, "The November 4 Vote for President: What Did It Mean?" p. 249.

3. Michael Barone and Grant Ujifusa, *The Almanac of American Politics: 1986* (Washington, D.C.: National Journal, 1987), "A Nation at Peace," p. xxxix.

4. Courtesy of Government Research Corporation, Washington, D.C.

5. John Maynard Keynes, *General Theory* (New York: Harcourt, Brace & World, 1964), p. 129.

6. Norman Ornstein, *Essays in Contemporary Economic Problems: The Economy in Deficit, 1985,* Philip Cagan, ed. (Washington, D.C.: American Enterprise Institute, 1985), "The Politics of the Deficit," pp. 313–14.

7. Thomas Wander, *Congress and the Presidency,* Vol. 9, No. 2, (Autumn 1982), "Patterns of Change in the Congressional Budget Process, 1865–1975," p. 48.

8. Ornstein, op. cit., p. 315.

9. Ibid.

10. Ibid., p. 316.

11. Ibid.

12. Ibid., p. 317.

13. Ibid., p. 318.

14. Ibid., p. 330.

15. Ibid., p. 331.

16. "Hoover Power Plant Act of 1984," P.L. 98-381.

17. P. G. Wodehouse, *The Mating Season* (New York: Didier Publishers, 1949), Chapter 22, p. 215.

18. Speech by Senator Ernest F. Hollings, "Making Government Work," delivered December 4, 1982, at Hilton Head, South Carolina, to the National Black Caucus of State Legislators.

19. Senator Daniel Patrick Moynihan, Britannica Lecture, September 12, 1986, "The 'New Science of Politics' Vindicated or The Founders Re-Discovered," given at the Woodrow Wilson Center, Smithsonian Institution, Washington, D.C.

20. Ibid.

21. *Economic Report of the President*, 1986, Table B-5, p. 259.

22. Moynihan, op. cit.

23. David A. Stockman, *The Triumph of Politics: How/Why the Reagan Revolution Failed* (New York: Harper & Row, 1986), p. 8.

24. Ibid., p. 10.

25. Ibid., p. 376.

26. Ibid., p. 9.

27. Ibid., p. 407.

28. Ibid., p. 409.

29. Secretary James Baker: Speech given to Houston Chamber of Commerce on May 14, 1985.

30. Ronald Reagan, "An Interview with the President," *Fortune*, September 21, 1981, p. 71.

31. Professor Samuel H. Beer, "The National Idea in American Politics," O'Neill Lecture, Boston College, April 21, 1982.

32. Abraham Lincoln, *The Collected Works of Abraham Lincoln, Vol. IV, 1860–1861*, Roy P. Basler, ed. (New Brunswick, New Jersey, Rutgers University Press, 1953), "The First Inaugural Address," March 4, 1861, p. 271.

## DEMOCRATS

1. Dean Acheson, *A Democrat Looks at His Party* (New York: Harper and Brothers, 1955), Chapter 1, pp. 11–12.

2. "Analysis Paper," in Horace W. Busby and Associates, *The Busby Papers* (Washington, D.C.) Vol. V-12, November 5, 1985, p. 2.

3. Nelson Polsby, *The American Elections of 1984*, Austin Ranney, ed. (Durham, North Carolina: Duke University Press, 1985), "The Democratic Nomination and the Evolution of the Party System," pp. 39–43.

4. Everett Carll Ladd, Senior Editor, *Public Opinion*, American Enterprise Institute, and Executive Director and President of The Roper Center for Public Opinion Research, University of Connecticut, in an interview with the author.

5. William Schneider, "The New Shape of American Politics," *The Atlantic Monthly*, January, 1987, p. 46.

6. Richard Brookhiser, *The Outside Story: How Democrats and Republicans Re-elected Reagan* (Garden City, New York: Doubleday & Company, Inc., 1986), p. 31.

7. Shakespeare, *Hamlet*, Act III, Scene 2, Lines 383 ff.

8. David Osborne, "Registration Boomerang: The Democrats Delivered the Republican Vote," *The New Republic*, February 25, 1985, p. 16.

9. Horace W. Busby and Associates, Trend Paper, January 8, 1987.

10. Michael Barone and Grant Ujifusa, *The Almanac of American Politics: 1982* (Washington, D.C.: Barone & Company, 1981), "New York," p. 723.

11. Arthur M. Schlesinger, Jr., *The Cycles of American History* (Boston: Houghton Mifflin Company, 1986), Chapter 2, p. 23.

12. Ibid., pp. 33–34.

13. Alan Brinkley, *The New Republic*, December 1, 1986, from a review of Arthur M. Schlesinger, Jr.'s *The Cycles of American History*, p. 28.

14. Schlesinger, op. cit., p. 29.

15. John Sears, in an interview with the author, August 29, 1985.

16. Schneider, op. cit., p. 44.

17. Ibid.

18. David Broder, *The Washington Post*, May 23, 1986.

19. Peter D. Hart, Geoffrey Garin, "Winning the White House: The Political Dynamics of 1988," paper published by Peter D. Hart Research Associates, Washington, D. C., February 1987, p. 2.

20. Ibid., p. 3.

21. Pat Caddell, "The Politics of the Baby Boom," in *Left, Right & Baby Boom: America's New Politics*, David Boaz, ed. (Washington, D.C.: Cato Institute, 1986), p. 42.

22. Peter D. Hart, in an interview with the author.

23. Ralph Whitehead, Jr., "The New Middle Americans," *New Perspectives Quarterly*, Vol. 2, Fall 86, p. 44.

24. Whitehead, press release issued at meeting of the Democratic Policy Commission, July 10, 1985.

25. Whitehead, in an interview with the author, April 28, 1987.

26. Whitehead, "New Collar Americans and the Democratic Vision," paper read to the Democratic Policy Commission, Washington, D.C., July 10, 1985.

27. Whitehead, in an interview with the author, April 28, 1987.

28. Hart, Garin, op. cit., p. 4.

29. Richard M. Scammon, Ben J. Wattenberg, *The Real Majority: An Extraordinary Examination of the American Electorate* (New York: Coward-McCann, Inc., 1970).

30. Ibid., Chapter 1, p. 21.

31. Ibid., Chapter 16, p. 225.

32. Ibid., Chapter 1, p. 20.

33. Ibid., Chapter 7, p. 95.

34. Ibid., Chapter 7, p. 97.

35. Ibid., Chapter 12, p. 168.

36. Robert D. Squier, President, Communications Company, Washington, D. C., in an interview with the author.

37. Scammon, Wattenberg, op. cit., Chapter 19, p. 275.

38. *New Choices in a Changing America: The Report of the Democratic Policy Commission to the Democratic National Committee,* August 1986, Democratic National Committee; Governor Scott M. Matheson, Chairman of the Commission, Chapter 1, p. 7.

39. Ibid., Introduction, p. 1.

40. Ibid., Chapter 1, p. 8.

41. Ibid., Chapter 3, p. 34.

42. Daniel Seligman, "Keeping Up," *Fortune,* November 12, 1984, p. 203.

43. William Schneider, "Trends in American Politics," in *Left, Right & Baby Boom,* op. cit., note 21, Chapter 1, p. 15.

44. Michael Barone, "Beyond Liberal and Conservative," ibid., Chapter 4, p. 79.

45. Terry Nichols Clarke, "Beyond Liberal and Conservative," ibid., Chapter 4, p. 90.

46. Paul Weaver, "Ideas in American Politics," ibid., Chapter 5, p. 97.

47. William Bradley, U.S. Senator, in an interview with the author.

48. William A. Henry III, *Visions of America: How We Saw the 1984 Election* (Boston/New York: The Atlantic Monthly Press, 1985), p. 51.

49. Irving Kristol, "New York Intellectuals," *The Washington Times,* Book Section, April 7, 1986.

50. Paul Hollander, *Political Pilgrims* (New York: Harper Colophon Books, 1983), p. 234.

51. Ibid., p. 236.

52. Ibid., p. 240.

53. Ibid., p. 245.

54. Lord Salisbury to Lord Lytton, June 15, 1877.

55. *New Choices in a Changing America,* op. cit., Chapter 6, "Making It Work," p. 65.

56. Ibid., Chapter 6, p. 56.

57. Ibid., Chapter 6, p. 59.

58. Ibid., Chapter 6, p. 62.

59. Ibid., Chapter 6, p. 61.

60. Ibid., Chapter 6, p. 65.

61. William R. Van Cleave, "The Chimera of Equitable Arms Control," *Global Affairs,* Vol. 1, Issue 1, Winter 1986, p. 22.

62. Walter Lippmann, *U.S. Foreign Policy: Shield of the Republic* (Boston: Little, Brown & Co., 1943), p. 55.

63. Sir Michael Howard, C.B.E., Regius Professor of Modern History at Oxford, in a speech delivered to The Woodrow Wilson International Center for Scholars, Washington, D.C., March 27, 1984.

64. Iain Elliott, "Reading, Writing and Rifle Drill," *London Times,* Editorial page, April 1, 1985.

65. Ibid.

66. Daniel Patrick Moynihan, "The Potemkin Palace," *The National Interest,* Number 2, Winter 1985/6, p. 91.

67. Henry S. Rowen, "Living with a Sick Bear," *The National Interest,* ibid., p. 25.

68. Ibid., p. 22.

69. Morton Kondracke, "Rainbow's End," *The New Republic,* April 30, 1984, p. 7.

70. Glenn C. Loury, Under-Secretary of Education (former Professor at the John F. Kennedy School of Government, Harvard University), "The Moral Quandary of the Black Community," *The Public Interest,* Number 79, Spring 1985, p. 14.

71. Ibid., p. 10.

72. Thomas E. Cavanagh, "The Impact of the Black Electorate," Election '84, Report #1 (Washington, D.C.: Joint Center for Political Studies, 1984), p. 5.

73. Lyndon Baines Johnson, Commencement Address on June 4, 1965, at Howard University, Washington, D.C.

74. Samuel P. Huntington, "The Visions of the Democratic Party," *The Public Interest*, Spring 1985, p. 66.

75. Abraham Lincoln, *The Collected Works of Abraham Lincoln, Vol. II, 1848–1858*, Roy P. Basler, ed. (New Brunswick, New Jersey, Rutgers University Press, 1953), "Dred Scott Decision," July 10, 1858, p. 495.

76. Barone and Ujifusa, *The Almanac of American Politics: 1984*, op. cit., "The Presidency," p. xxix.

77. Joseph Epstein, "True Virtue," *New York Times Magazine*, November 24, 1985, p. 64.

78. Ibid.

79. Ibid.

80. Ibid.

81. Ibid.

82. John Updike, *Bech Is Back* (New York: Fawcett, 1982), p. 15.

83. Pete Du Pont, from an interview with the author published in *Newsweek*, December 22, 1986.

84. William Schneider, "The New Shape of American Politics," *The Atlantic Monthly*, January 1987, p. 50.

## CONCLUSION

1. Peter De Vries, *I Hear America Swinging* (Boston: Little, Brown and Co., 1976), p. 120.

2. Robert Nisbet, *Prejudices: A Philosophical Dictionary* (Cambridge, Massachusetts: Harvard University Press, 1982), "Boredom," p. 23.

3. Richard M. Scammon, Ben J. Wattenberg, *The Real Majority: An Extraordinary Examination of the American Electorate* (New York: Coward-McCann, Inc., 1970), Chapter 18, "Complications," p. 273.

4. Daniel Patrick Moynihan, *Counting Our Blessings: Reflections on the Future of America* (Boston: The Atlantic Monthly Press/Little Brown and Co., 1980), "The Iron Law of Emulation," p. 117.

5. Ibid., p. 119.

6. William A. Henry III, *Visions of America: How We Saw the 1984 Election* (Boston/New York: The Atlantic Monthly Press, 1985), p. 3.

7. Scammon, Wattenberg, op. cit., Part Two, Chapter 2, "Tide Watching," p. 26.

8. Theodore H. White, *America in Search of Itself: The Making of the President 1956–1980* (New York: Harper & Row, 1982), "Interpassage: Ideas in Motion," p. 101.

9. Ibid., "The Reign of Television," p. 185.

10. Arthur Miller, *The Price* (New York: Viking Inc., 1968), p. 41.

11. Saul Bellow, *Mr. Sammler's Planet* (New York: Viking Press, 1970), p. 228.

12. Michael Barone and Grant Ujifusa, *The Almanac of American Politics: 1982* (Washington, D.C.: Barone & Company, 1982), "The Presidency," p. xxi.

# INDEX

214

# About the Author

George F. Will's syndicated column appears in more than 400 newspapers. He is also a regular contributing editor to *Newsweek,* providing the back-page essay twice a month. In 1977, he won a Pulitzer Prize for commentary in his newspaper columns. Mr. Will was for seven years a regular panelist on "Agronsky & Company" and is currently a news analyst for *ABC News.* He is also a panelist on *ABC*'s "This Week with David Brinkley." Mr. Will is the author of *The Pursuit of Happiness and Other Sobering Thoughts, The Pursuit of Virtue and Other Tory Notions, Statecraft as Soulcraft* and *The Morning After: American Successes and Excesses, 1981–86.*

Mr. Will was born in Champaign, Illinois. He was educated at Trinity College, Hartford, Connecticut; Magdalen College, Oxford University (B.A., Politics, Philosophy and Economics); and Princeton University (Ph.D., Politics).